PLAYIN' TO Win

A **SURGEON, SCIENTIST** and **PARENT** examines the **UPSIDE** of VIDEO GAMES

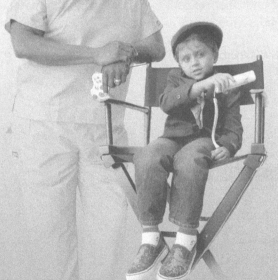

JAMES "BUTCH" ROSSER, MD, FACS

www.playintowin.com

NEW YORK

PLAYIN' TO WIN

A **SURGEON**, **SCIENTIST** and **PARENT** examines the *UPSIDE* OF **VIDEO GAMES**

www.playintowin.com

JAMES "BUTCH" ROSSER, MD, FACS

ISBN: 978-1-60037-361-9 (Paperback)
ISBN: 978-1-60037-362-6 (Hardcover)
ISBN: 978-1-60037-363-3 (Audio)

Published by:

MORGAN · JAMES
THE ENTREPRENEURIAL PUBLISHER™
www.morganjamespublishing.com

Morgan James Publishing, LLC

1225 Franklin Ave. Ste 325

Garden City, NY 11530-1693

Toll Free 800-485-4943

www.MorganJamesPublishing.com

Habitat
for Humanity®
Peninsula
Building Partner

Book jacket photography and design by:
Chris Soria

Interior layout and design by:
Bonnie Bushman
bbushman@bresnan.net

DEDICATION

This book is dedicated to the most important people in my life including:

- My maternal grandparents, Ludie and Pearl Mitchell, and parents James and Marjorie Rosser who instilled within me a belief that this country would always recognize a hard worker and a well-placed heart.

- My wife, Dana. With her support and inner strength I am alive to share my thoughts with you.

- My children, Kevin, Duane, Nicole, Taylor and Tianna for their presence and support, which helped me to continue writing when I wanted to give up.

- This book is also written in honor of every child or adult who succeed in spite of the system, and to those who were lost because of the system. May their sacrifices not be in vain!

ACKNOWLEDGEMENTS

To Eric Eisenhart, Debra Tilson, Dawn Mitchell, Paul Wetter, M.D. and his wife Janis, Karen N. Peart, for editing, Adrian Knight, Wayman Armstrong, Bjorn Herman, M.D., George Kalergis, Julie Johnson, Chris Soria, Stacy L'Air Lee-Eaisley, Angela Nicole Sumlin, Bishop James Dixon, Bishop Joey Johnson, Pastor Kerry Shook and staff, and countless others who directly contributed or indirectly offered inspiration that made this book possible.

FOREWORD

By Dr. Rod Paige
Former United States Secretary of Education, 2001-2005

Throughout nature, in almost every form of higher life, play represents a joyous way to learn and practice life skills. We can all recall images of bear cubs, as just one example from nature, practicing with each other the hunting skills that will allow them to survive as adults. Dr. Rosser explores how that often repeated example in nature can be harnessed for not just our children but for adults as well. This thoughtful exploration comes not a moment too soon.

To insist that all learning takes place inside a classroom is simply foolish. To turn our backs on activities that children are naturally drawn to is equally shortsighted. Here then, is both an innovative and common sense approach to bringing together our desire and need to better educate our children and the natural tendency of children to play.

Today, computer games can be found in almost every American home where children are present. Parents worry that the "addictive" nature of such play can command the rapt fascination of children far beyond their normal attention spans. For many, this activity is considered "mindless" entertainment. But does it have to be?

Without a doubt, there are a wide range of video games that, like food itself, span a spectrum between junk food that might be tasty but which is not really very good for you, to foods that provide essential nutrition for growth as well as energy—and yes, pleasure. So too, is the world of video games. While many (too many some would rightfully say) focus only on "shoot 'em up" scenarios, there are also excellent games on the market, carefully designed for each age level, that actually contain a tremendous amount of useful, interesting and perhaps otherwise unseen information that in the context of "play" become fascinating to children.

Can a game that requires the player to understand the history of dinosaurs, for example, have the effect of equipping that child with a body of knowledge about dinosaurs that would only be learned with much greater difficulty from a text? Yes. As explored in this book, children naturally love play and if the requirement of that play is learning ideas and facts in order to "win," then learning becomes great fun. This kind of learning can represent a base of knowledge that can then be built upon in the classroom and at home. Adapted to a more formal education setting, learning through play can even transform the tedium and drudgery of learning by rote into joyous and robust participation by children.

The key here is the "food" for the mind as contained in the games. Popcorn, cotton candy and soft drinks make up probably most of the computer games on the market and many that so cavalierly employ graphic violence represent "poisons" for the young mind. These games teach, too, but lessons that undermine both the individual and society as a whole.

There are also games that are wonderfully inventive, full of interesting facts, history and details, graphically expressed in a game context. More importantly, the methodology of video game design and the intoxicating participatory allure offer a blueprint that could help construct an education system that is a juggernaut which inspires and delivers real "nutritional value" for K-16 students and beyond.

Should computer gaming replace hearty play in a park, backyard or playground? No, obviously not. Social skills, physical activity and the unbridled joy of physical exuberance won't be easily found on a computer screen. But in the 21st century it would also be shortsighted not to recognize the potential that such a medium has for making learning not only fun but also compelling. When "mindless" entertainment turns into cerebral entertainment much progress can be made.

Today a greater and greater percentage of our children have disconnected from traditional school settings and dropout rates and undesirable social activities have grown proportionally. No society can long survive the number of children who are failing in our public schools today. If educational and fun computer gaming can provide us one more tool to connect children with the joys of learning, we should not run from the idea but embrace it. Games that begin to build a base of knowledge that will later inspire children to embrace medicine, the arts, science and math can do wonders to transform "book learning" into dynamic and challenging interactions between children and a body of knowledge.

This book explores what may be the leading edge in a revolution in modern learning—harnessing the natural enthusiasm children have for play with the necessity to better educate and equip our children for our changing and challenging modern world.

I want to apologize for my unabashed focus on the impact on education that this book has set the stage for. But my first love has been and shall always be education. It is indeed hard to "teach an old dog new tricks." Please do not mistake my attentiveness as a sign of neglect to the much broader implications that this book brings to light. I have had the privilege of sitting on the boards of several major corporations and I am privy to their most guarded concerns. They all are struggling with how they are going to attract, cultivate and harvest today's "next gen" kids to be a formidable work force that can "play to win" in a competitive, hostile global environment. The introduction of video game-induced "stealth learning" into corporate training could provide some of the answers they seek.

I have also had the honor of being in the cabinet of the commander-in-chief of our great nation and I have had an eagle's view of the expanse of concerns that confront our nation. It is quite clear that the content of this book has deep penetrating relevance to successfully addressing many of our nation's woes.

I am particularly struck by Dr. Rosser's approach to leveraging the learning potential in video games as an asset to put our nation's citizens in a position to help heal themselves. Truly, this change in tradition promises to confront the crisis that we face in providing medical coverage for all citizens of this country. Butch has it right, the future of our republic hinges on how well we empower ordinary people to accomplish extraordinary things. To paraphrase the mantra of the great state of Ohio, "education is the heart of it all."

TABLE of CONTENTS

TABLE of CONTENTS

• • • •

PREFACE

There is a revolution brewing. You might not know that it is a revolution because the weapons of this revolution aren't guns or rockets. It doesn't involve overthrowing governments. It is a revolution about overthrowing worshiped, outdated institutions and the way they do business. Our country is in trouble, and when a great nation like the United States of America is in decline, it is up to its citizens to do something about it. We have the responsibility to rise up and insist on the radical evolution of all the major social institutions in our country—schools, churches, healthcare and even corporate America.

And one of the main weapons for change…are you ready for this?… video games. No, you didn't misread—video games. Those electronic toys that many people love to play and others love to hate because they've been touted as the downfall of all humankind.

My name is Dr. James Rosser—"Butch" to those who know me. And I am on a mission. I want to help establish a foundation of credibility and legitimacy for the incorporation of video games into the mainstream to address pressing societal issues. I'm using this book, *Playin' To Win* as a vehicle to introduce you to my mission and to build excitement about climbing aboard what myself and others call the "Games-4-Good" movement. This movement hinges on an effort to recruit video games and other pop culture icons to become assets that can contribute to the formulization of solutions to difficult challenges confronting our nation.

This book is written for every child that has sat in a classroom and been forced to come up with creative survival techniques to tolerate the onslaught of a monotone, uninspired teacher or professor who was hell bent on taking them through compulsory and out-of-touch lesson plans.

Many became casualties of "friendly fire." victims of "the system," and history will never chronicle their names. These students were not able to survive because they could not stay in the game. They perished because they couldn't connect the dots that revealed the image of the big picture. They failed to come up with a credible answer to the question, "why do I have to know that?"

This book is for every parent who has lain awake at night, worrying about what the future holds for their precious children in a world that presents so many influences and distractions. I hope they hear this message: "There is hope and it is going to be okay!"

This book is for every politician who has struggled to make a decision to restrict or even censure video games because on the surface they seem harmful to the public, but harsh action would provide a short-lived political advantage. It is for every educator who has wanted to step outside of the box of rubber stamped lesson plans filed with bureaucratic rhetoric, only to be beat down by superiors who were blindly committed to the status quo.

This book is meant to trumpet a call for the empowerment of the people by all means necessary. I want this book to be the birth certificate for a revolution that embraces rather than shuns pop culture, a revolution that eradicates fear through scientific evaluation and validation, a revolution that will be fought from the top down and the bottom up. From the waltz, the telephone, radio, the movies, Rock-n-Roll, Hip Hop and Rap, and now to video games, pop culture has never readily accepted and efficiently incorporated video games into mainstream society.

As with any disruptive innovation, there is always a predictable response of fear, over-exaggerated calls for alarm, unsuccessful attempts at censorship, rejection and even eradication. Now is the time to break that cycle.

Pop culture is a child of society and good can be found in every child. Like a loving parent, society must identify the good in its offspring and nurture it. Let's not be guilty of abusing a child with so much potential. And we should do this with the knowledge that we do not have the luxury of gradual intervention.

We are facing a crisis in our educational system; millions of our children are underachieving. If our children are not motivated to engage in the learning process, and if process participation does not translate into real world relevance, our great American culture is "kaput."

Because it is so crucial to the cause of revitalizing our nation, this book is not meant to be hidden away in the education or textbook section of the library or bookstore. It is not meant to be placed in your elephant graveyard of book titles stacked in a corner. I hope you will spill coffee in it because what you read shocks or thrills you with the expanse of its possibilities.

I want you to use this book as a resource that you can turn to again and again, not only for reference, but also for inspiration and entertainment. This book is a fervent reminder that change, especially when it is connected to something of significance, is not accomplished by pure intellect that resides within your cranial vault, but rather victory is ultimately dependent upon that which resides within your heart.

Finally, this book is absolutely not meant to be some self-salvation for the world. It is what it is—One man's attempt to assist in the establishment of a credible hope that has the potential to shape a planet with a future that will be greater than its past.

To make our future great, we need to revolutionize the way we educate, train and empower our citizens. To make any revolution successful, we must all select a part—big or small—where we can get busy making contributions.

In the book *The Tipping Point,* Malcolm Gladwell used an example of the power of a social epidemic to spark the resurgence of Hush Puppies® shoes in American and global fashion. If a social epidemic can help turn Hush Puppies around, maybe applying some of the same principles could lead the empowerment revolution to cross a threshold, tip and spread like wildfire. As in all successful revolutions, unlikely alliances must be formed, and past enemies must embrace. Let's get rid of secrecy and closed mindedness; open sharing and collaboration must be held sacred. If you are reluctant to join because you are uncomfortable with an intimate proximity with protest, my response is inspired from a message by Martin Luther King Jr.: "Each participant in the struggle must become familiar with peaceful protest."

For those among you willing to participate in the struggle, protesting the 'status quo' by offering up this unconventional solution of using video games on the frontline of learning, must become as familiar as breathing. Do you think about breathing? No, you just do it. Your moment-to-moment contribution to this campaign for change must at all times be directed to *Playin' To Win*.

INTRODUCTION:
FORGING A NEW FRONTIER

When I was a child, I loved going to a new places. There was always a collage of mixed emotions that gave the experience a memorable ambience. This book represents a new place for me, and a new direction for everyone. It is a power-packed exploration of video game pop culture, and I want to show how we can harness it as an energy source to propel a declining nation that has strayed from its competitive roots back into a respected global leadership role. It explores the hazy boundaries of a new frontier.

This book does not stop at supplying suggestions based on conjecture; it offers hard scientific data and real-world for-instances. It looks at the history and relevance of the $40 billion dollar video game industry and lays the foundation for the recognition of its legitimacy. The message is carried in a unique matrix of substance, facts and southern story telling, meant to connect the minds and hearts of a nation.

This book provides the spiritual loincloth of a movement to embrace video games in mainstream society and put them on the frontline of the battle to save the American dream.

I am a surgeon and scientist by training and a social advocate at heart. In the first part of the book I share why I decided to step out of my area of expertise and contribute to a social cause—salvaging education and championing the concept of "learning for empowerment." In this way, I guess that I'm an activist. I am also a parent who just happens to be an avid video game player. My personal legacy with video games and pop culture has long assisted in my personal and professional development. This gives me a unique vantage point, and from that vantage point, I have come to believe with all my heart that video games can be used for good.

From my research as a surgeon and scientist, I also fundamentally understand how to leverage these "digital dynamos" to address our nation's problems in education, healthcare and beyond.

Within the pages of this book, I make a diagnosis that may be startling to some. This nation is suffering from a terminal disease called "malignant performance malaise." This is a medical symptom characterized by feeling sluggish and weak. You know something is wrong, but you don't know what. It is usually a sign of an underlying disease that has not fully manifested itself. The United States is performing sluggishly and is displaying signs of weakness. And, just as with my patients, if a diagnosis is not identified and treated promptly, death will ensue. So shall be the fate of this country.

The death of the United States as a supreme superpower is inevitable if adjustments are not made. Part one of the book gives details of the signs and symptoms that support this diagnosis. It also discusses how the prescribed treatment regimen— a return to a heritage of competition and winning, combined with video games—can be the key to a cure.

After I present a diagnosis of the problem, I present a case for a cure based on solutions provided by the business and economic worlds, and how various facets of video game capability and culture will play an important role in this heroic turnaround effort. But while I have confidence that I have captured your attention at this point, I realize that there are some who might not be convinced and will continue to struggle to accept my idea. To address these concerns, I provide scientific data to justify the book's bold contentions as to why video games will anchor a nation's comeback.

I begin by specifically addressing the problems that prejudices for and against video games create. Prejudice, as a barrier of resistance, must be addressed, controlled, and hopefully eradicated.

Video games are a frequently misunderstood pop culture icon. My mission is to shed light on their true profile, and being a scientist, I provide details of science and historical facts surrounding both the pros and cons of video games. I give both sides in order to empower everyone to evaluate for themselves the current and future tidal wave of studies and articles that will be generated about video games and their long-term effects on children and adults. Most importantly, I want readers to be aware of the data that exists because the ability to critically evaluate and determine whether presentations of conclusions are based on sound scientific principles, will be critical in the near future because of the tornado of investigations forming around video games.

Video game developers continue to push the envelope by putting sexually explicit and extremely violent materials in their titles—political conflict is unavoidable. If we are going to use video games as tools to revolutionize our educational system, we all must be prepared to assist our elected officials in making sound decisions.

Social and cultural critics have long observed that political systems, including our own, have repeatedly force-fed the agenda "of a few on the many." For the most part, video games are seen as too violent and overly sexual and therefore many see censorship as a shortcut to a solution. But in the end, censorship is not an option, especially when it is used as a quick fix to pacify public concern. It is a line in the sand that must not be crossed. If video games are to successfully navigate the treacherous and serpentine road to legitimacy and mainstream acceptance, the public must have a handle on the good, the bad, and the ugly.

Next, I make the case that it is imperative that the good characteristics of video games be incorporated into the core institutions of this nation—homes, schools and churches. It is this core that must be healed. I present guidelines and strategies to provide a beacon for those who volunteer to carry the flag of implementation. Finally, I present case studies that detail how fearless explorers have shown us how video games, instead of creating more problems, can tackle and solve real world issues.

This book is inspired, in part, by many edgy titles that have previously probed the expanse of what could be in our future. It is a "Freakanomics" with a more grassroots subject matter that elicits an instantaneous visceral response from citizens from all walks of life. It is an *Everything Bad Is Good For You* with more gritty details on how the unexpected can be incorporated into raising our society to another level. Ultimately, it makes a case that video games can promote a *Tipping Point* with a focus on contributing to societal solutions. This book is direct, thought provoking and consistently challenges perceptions of the boundaries of reality. I want readers to be among the first to bear witness to this call for the start of a second American Revolution!

Part One

SETTiNG
THE STAGE

● ● ● ●

I have always loved hearing the story behind anything that is of substance. Understanding how and why someone or something becomes successful has always intrigued me. I guess that is why I love history. It is the sheet music of the struggle of a world to evolve toward the unreachable goal of being a perfect place to live. Being a Southerner, I also love the art form of story telling. This section is the story behind who, what and why I choose to write this book. It is a history of what has inspired me to step out of my comfort zone and participate in a revolution.

CHAPTER ONE
THE LiTTLE VOiCE WiTH NO FACE

When I was 12 years old, I felt that I was ready to proclaim an intimate relationship with God. It was time for a public proclamation — the tradition of the black Southern Baptist Church. From birth, the Church and faith have always been a part of my life. I went to church for the first time when I was one week old. Twelve years later, revival week had come, and I felt that I was ready to go through the one-week ritual that was meant to publicly announce your personal resolve to such a serious commitment. The revival lasted from Monday to Friday and required full participation for all five days in order to become eligible to be baptized. There were absolutely no exceptions, and tardiness was not tolerated.

On Wednesday of that week, I had a conflicting activity and when I got home my mother had already gone to the church. I had to bathe, dress and get there, all in 40 minutes. My bike was broken, so the only way I could get to the church on time was by taking my brother Chuck's bicycle without his permission. I dressed and got on Chuck's bike and pedaled faster than I had ever done before. I got there with two minutes to spare.

During the sermon, my heart was not at peace because I had taken my brother's bike without permission, and here I was on public display proclaiming my commitment to caring, character and service. I began crying on the ride back home because of what I had done. My tears blurred my vision and all of a sudden, I hit something in the road and fell into a ditch. I must have struck my head because I sensed myself lying in the most comfortable bed I had ever experienced and a soft, low voice was coming from an amorphous shape that had no face. The decibels of the voice were muted, but I could feel each word reverberate through my body. It was so comforting. The voice told me that everything was going to be alright.

I woke up in the ditch with an intense headache that quickly went away. As I picked myself up, I may have looked the same on the outside, but I left that ditch a different person. I did not see a burning bush and the red sea did not part, but I got up knowing that I had a purpose. I knew that I would be called upon someday to lead and I had to be ready.

Today, the little voice with no face is challenging me to take on my most seemingly impossible task to date. I am being compelled to step out of my familiar role of contributing to society one person at a time and impact an arena that, on the surface, I have no skill set for—the arena of social change. For you see, I have always been reluctant, at first, to take up the challenges presented to me.

By training, I am a surgical healer. I am able to eliminate threats to a person's well-being by extracting and correcting disease with minimal invasion to the body. I have received many awards of distinction from around the globe for my efforts. Yet, I never wanted to be surgeon. Truth be known, as I have achieved the successes that the public sees, it has been done with me as an unlikely participant. I have always been a stubborn, unwilling, and yes, a reluctant hero. Perhaps it is because I have been intimately aware that the price of leadership and success has always been expensive and it requires payment from those other than yourself, such as family, friends, and sometimes even your faith.

When I began contemplating taking up this challenge of making video games, the center point of educational reform, I found myself asking, "Why should anyone want to leave the safe confines of their comfort zone?" "What makes an individual depart the established landscape of their lives, which they have spent a lifetime grooming?" "What makes a person get out of their rocking chairs on the front porch and leave their yards to find and develop a new property?" "Why am I now, in middle age, crossing over into pop culture to use it for the greater good?" "Why change my life when it is so very good?"

After much self-examination, the most compelling reason for me to venture into unknown territory is to flee from an enemy called "average."

As I struggled for expanded clarification, my wife helped by giving me John L. Mason's book, *An Enemy Called Average*. She is always finding ways to help her needy life partner, and Mason's book was just the ticket. It offers riveting reflections that may seem small but can lead to big life changes. Like a prospector in the California gold rush of old, I searched this book for golden nuggets of advice that would help guide me in making an accurate decision tailored for the situation I faced. And did I make some great finds!

My favorites begin with nugget #35, "when you refuse to change; you end up in chains." Then nugget #28, "those that do not take chances do not make advances." This was followed by nugget #8, "the best time of the day is now." I am really fond of nugget #2, "the only place to start is where you are." This is followed by nugget #44, "everything big starts with something little." Another favorite is nugget #60, "stand for what is right, then even if you lose, you win." I fell in love with nugget #65, "retreat to advance." But, the final golden nugget of advice that I found in this great book was nugget #71, "do what's right, the right way, at the right time." These eight illustrious bits of wisdom had a laser-like alignment with the quandary that I found myself in. And they would serve to give me the confidence to risk it all, and shift the focus of my life.

When an individual sets out to address a seemingly unsolvable problem, there must be strong driving forces causing them to willingly walk into a darkened abyss. What I am setting out to do seems like entering an abyss. I have no track record of being a social activist for the masses. I am a healer trained to help one person at a time. I am reminded of a scene in the movie *Top Gun*, when "Maverick" and "Goose" are involved in a dogfight with another airplane. Fighter pilots call this a one-v (versus) one engagement, where it is just you against the other guy. With unbridled confidence, Maverick embarks on executing a risky maneuver in the hopes of getting a kill. "Goose," ever cautious in the back seat, proclaimed with belligerent protest, "Hey Mav, we don't have any fuel for this." I asked myself the same question; "do I have what it takes to pull this off?"

To let readers be the judge of that, I will provide some further background information about myself. I am 53 years old, and I am a living testimony and poster child product of pop culture. I was able to read on a sixth grade level at the age of six because I read Marvel comic books. My first desire to become a doctor was fertilized by my love of the TV show *Ben Casey, M.D.* Since I have become a doctor I have contributed to the care of people around the world. I often use technology in innovative ways to bring treatment to those who are in the greatest need. My interest in computers and technology was established by watching *The Jetsons*.

I also have seasoned life experiences that dictate my intervention while serving as a profound force that drives me. I write this book not because I want to be a hero, but because of fear. I have fear of the future. Without corrective measures, I am afraid we will lose an opportunity to put our nation in a position to maintain its global influence in the future.

I know what it is like to live in fear. I grew up in Moorhead, Mississippi, a small town in the Delta at the height of Jim Crow segregation and the civil rights movement. I could not drink out of the same fountain as many of my readers, and my parents put their lives on the line to exercise the right to vote. Despite my daily intimate dance with fear, desperation and survival, my belief in this social experiment called the United States of America, never faltered. I believed, like my father before me and his father before him, that in spite of its imperfections, it was a blessing that we could call ourselves citizens of this great nation.

In Jim Crow Mississippi, back in the 1960s, this state of mind was aggressively tested. In the midst of these turbulent times, a show called *Star Trek* came on the scene to provide vivid imagery and dialogue as to how our society should be. If the creators and sponsors of this show were bold enough to portray a white American starship captain sharing the bridge with a Russian, an African American woman, and an alien named Spock, surely it would not be long before the unenlightened and misguided in this great nation would see the error in their systematic discrimination of others based on the color of their skin.

I have always been inspired by the vision of Dr. Martin Luther King, Jr. because in times like these, patience and productivity is the order of the day. If we are productive; if we all rise up and answer the call of duty to do whatever we can to make this world better, then we will see the fruition of Dr. King's dream for America. He always felt that the winds of change are inevitable, and once they start they are unstoppable.

So with this background, I write this book to answer the call to go beyond that which I feel comfortable in doing. In spite of my feelings of profound inadequacy, it is time to saddle up and "get 'er done."

Playin' To Win is meant to provide a road map and vehicle that will mobilize an effort leading to the recruitment of our nation's expanding pool of untapped human resources. This will empower a renaissance of innovation. This cultural transformation will be based on upgrading our outdated educational system, and the proliferation of the spirit of collaborative competition.

I hope to present an effective argument, backed by data, that a popular culture icon called video games will fuel this renaissance. I am convinced that this ambitious endeavor can be accomplished if we use the due diligence of scientific investigation to identify, validate and deploy rarely-appreciated powerful, positive attributes of this unlikely ally.

With participation by the masses, diversity—the strength of our nation—will be harnessed as a newfound paradigm-shifting natural resource. This shall reclaim the countless individuals who have been systematically shut out or run out of mainstream society because of a chronic disconnect between how they are taught, how they learn, and how they become empowered to do what they like to do.

Can video games help us to educate our children better? Can they inspire and prepare them for career choices in such fields as science, technology, engineering, medicine and mathematics? Can entertainment be fused with education to empower a new generation through "stealth learning?" (Learning while having fun) Can the salvation and dream of healthcare for all be dependent upon our ability to incorporate video game applications into the education and therapeutic interventions of patients and providers? Can video games be used to enhance the moral fiber of a nation's citizens? Is it possible that I can really convince a skeptical public that something that they feel is bad, could contribute to the greater good? Is the key to several of the world's most perplexing dilemmas to be found among raw assets that others feel are frivolous demonstrations of wasteful efforts of humanity?

These are just a few of the questions I will attempt to answer in this book, and I am doing it because though I am eligible to be a member of AARP, I am still able. I don't believe that the exploration of new frontiers should be left to the young. So, just when I was beginning to think that I was ready to settle for being average, a "little voice with no face" calls to me to take up a noble crusade.

CHAPTER TWO

ᑌIDEO ᑕAMES! WHY ᑌIDEO ᑕAMES?

I know that some readers are thinking, "Is this guy nuts?" Here's a respectable surgeon who thinks that video games can be the fix to the problems in learning, education and individual empowerment. I have done a lot of research and I am the author of over one hundred scientific writings, including an article published in the February 2007 *Archives of Surgery*, one of the most respected peer reviewed surgical journals on the subject. I have run programs with suburban and inner-city children that use video games to teach them the basics of anatomy and surgery. And guess what? These kids love it!! Is this surprising? No! Because, the cold hard truth of the matter is that video games are simply an empowerment tool. It is what we do with them that make them bad or good.

Some of you might be protesting—even loudly—that video games could never be good for us! They're all full of sex and violence, aren't they? As I continued my research, my next revelation was that we are not at the mercy of these extraordinary forces. Yes, many of the video games out there are about death and destruction—and that carries with it the belief that these games are teaching our children to be death-minded and destruction-oriented—but that doesn't have to be.

From a scientist's perspective, it simply comes down to the fact that you can influence the outcome of video games by manipulating four variables: amount of play, subject matter, form of play, and mechanics of play. In short, video games are not, by definition, destructive and threatening to society. You can make them do anything that you want them to, and that includes using them as a tool to revolutionize our society.

One of the most impressive but troubling discoveries I have made about video games is the fact that they incorporate into their design many key findings of educational research that are "best practice" teaching techniques. There is a huge irony here—our educational system isn't using the very techniques that they have suggested work best. But video game developers leverage these assets all of the time in their titles.

Let's face it; our present system is just not cutting it. Kids are bored in school—but they don't have to be! There is also an appalling drop in students interested in science, technology engineering and mathematics, otherwise referred to as STEM. Video games can address how children are motivated to learn. They can create a perfect learning storm that truly will leave no child behind. I even convinced a Harvard Ph.D. in education to agree with me. Here's how I did it:

The Great Plane-Ride Debate

It was a typical hot, humid day in the land of Mickey— Orlando, Florida. I had just finished a visit with my best friend and I was flying to Boston to attend a medical conference. I was ecstatic because I had just been given a complementary first class seat. At 6' 4" and 290 pounds, this was truly a reason to celebrate. As I settled in with my iPod and began playing *Ms. Pacman*, a young lady asking to get to the window seat interrupted me. I smiled and said, "hello." I then asked whether she was going home or going to Boston for business. She said that she was going home. I followed up by asking what she did for a living, and she stated that she was a doctoral candidate at Harvard in education. Her life's goal was to train future educators. I told her my name and extended my hand. It was left loitering in mid-air as her eyebrows instantly became raised. "You are that guy who is saying that video games can be used for good aren't you?" she said. I hesitantly replied, "Y-y-yes." She then went into an extended emotional oration about how video games were universally bad and they were the main reason why children were doing poorly in school. She could not understand why a person of science would be so irresponsible as to put an academic effort into such a frivolous piece of subject matter.

I was completely caught off guard. My first response was to instinctively tear this person apart limb by limb with a verbal machete. I have a reputation for being a very notorious and lethal debater. Audiences around the globe have witnessed me carving my opponents up into pieces and displaying their carcasses to the crowd as they laughed at the comedic and entertaining nature of my assault tactics. But, as I looked down at this petite but passionate and brilliant young lady, I did not have the heart to unleash my customary brutal frontal attack. While I knew that I needed to ultimately deal a knock-out blow to her misguided prejudice, I decided to proceed in stealth mode.

I politely allowed her to get everything off her chest and I began my rebuttal in a soft, humble voice. First, I shared with her that all of this began as a personal journey to try to resolve a riveting scientific question in my mind: Can video games assist in training better surgeons? I also told her that I wanted to get a sense of whether video games have any positive benefits for society. I had a private interest in this effort because I am the father of five children and a grandfather. Her demeanor began to soften and she started to relax and her eyebrows returned to their normal position.

I continued by holding up my iPod with *Ms. Pacman* and told her that I did not want something that I practiced to wrongly influence my children to venture into harm's way. So, being a scientist, I became committed to using good old-fashioned research to identify the data that I needed to make valid conclusions. I confessed to her that even though my motives were selfish, I was at first hesitant to put the huge effort required into this research. But with great reluctance, I decided to forge on. I could tell my opening statement had accomplished its goal of softening her posture. She was leaning on her elbow and her chin was cupped in her hand. Then with unbridled interest she said, "What did you do next?"

I knew I had the high ground, so I became bolder. I ventured into her territory—educational research. I told her that I extensively reviewed both the video game and educational research literature. One of my areas of focus dealt with the developmental make-up of video games and the methodology of video game design. After reading this information, I agreed with the conclusions of many others that the impact of video game play could be manipulated by modulating the key components I mentioned earlier in this chapter: time, content, form, and mechanics of the interface. My conclusion was that all video games are not created equal, and we can extract the good from video games. I continued by giving more details on the four components.

The effect of the *amount* of game play is easy to understand. The amount of time exposed to any energy source has a very transparent cause and effect. If you stay out in the hot sun without protection you will become sunburned. If you are exposed to radioactive materials, you will undergo more harm the longer you are exposed. The flip side is that the more you are exposed to or practice something, the higher the possibility for mastery. Research in video game play and television viewing has shown that exposure to certain *content* can generate outcomes in children both bad and good. The positive impact of *Sesame Street* and its learning empowerment profile is a shining example of bench research harnessing a powerful pop culture icon for the greater good.

The realm of *form*, I continued, is much more difficult to grasp. Successful video game design is dependent upon the formal features of the game; how the graphics, sounds, challenges, scoring and rewards all come together to produce almost a trance-like immersion into the game. I used the video game on my iPod as an example. When playing *Ms. Pacman*, the hungry monster travels around a maze, eating dots as quickly as it can before other monsters higher up on the food chain eat it.

The developers could have used only visuals to set the stage of play, but this would not have been as immersive because of the lack of sound. The sound that accompanies the monster's movement enhances the sense of motion and speed. The gulping sound when each dot is consumed augments the feeling of accomplishment. The consumption of a power dot and the resultant change in sound, visuals and graphics heighten the feeling of accomplishment.

I was amazed to find how much the *mechanical* interface can influence the impact of playing the game on the individual. If you want a person to become a pilot while playing a video or computer game, you should use an airplane joystick that is similar to what a pilot uses. If you want your child to develop good driving skills from playing a video game, the mechanical interface to play the game should be a steering wheel similar to what is used to drive a car. The mouse or keyboard is suboptimal if real world skill-sets are to be transferred from the virtual environment.

I summarized my findings by driving home this most important point: the effect of video games on the lives of individuals is not predetermined, either bad or good. Individual outcomes can be modified depending on the ratio of key features of the game that the individual is exposed to, similar to a chemistry experiment.

I told my new friend that this last bit of data was a revelation of nuclear proportions for me because it placed the argument into the realm of science. I decided that as far as the impact of video games on an individual is concerned, video games could be identified or custom designed to not just entertain, but to also contribute to the greater good. My job as scientist and researcher, should be to identify the key elements in each game, apply them to a targeted application, pinpoint the proportion and morphology of the important variables, and validate the application with experimental due diligence.

As my voice fell silent, we both leaned back in our seats and stared forward, as if we had been running a sprint and stopped to take a break. For her, my story had suggested possibilities that she had previously not considered. For me, a fire that had been smoldering for quite some time had begun erupting into a flame. She turned to me and said, "Please tell me more."

Gosh, I Didn't Know That!

Whoa! I had made an impact on my adversary. I knew it from the way she requested more information. But I found myself caught in the emotional debris extracted by my argument. I could see that she was beginning to regret how our conversation started and the aggressive way she initially addressed me. I began feeling sorry for her and I asked myself if I was being too harsh. Naw, I don't think so! In an instant, I refocused. I had a debate to win; I could not go soft now. So I quickly regained my top debating form and began barraging her with information on the video game industry's prominence and influence in today's society.

In 2004, video games flew off shelves like bottle rockets on the fourth of July. That year, almost eight titles per second, per day, sold throughout the year. The U.S. video game market alone reached $20 to $25 billion in sales in 2007, with the projected worldwide market expected to grow to $46.5 billion by 2010. The Bureau of Labor Statistics predicts that the growth of software publishing, of which video games are a part, will expand by 67.9 percent between 2002 and 2012. The movie industry pales in comparison to video game revenue.

Halo 2, one of the best-selling titles of 2004, took in an estimated $263 million dollars in its first day of sales; more than any movie has ever taken in its opening day. A factor that will maintain this trend in the foreseeable future is that more and more movies are developing and selling video games to boost revenue from movie projects. Talk about the tail wagging the dog. Sales for the April-December period, representing the first nine months of Nintendo's 2006 fiscal year, saw a 73 percent increase to ¥712.6 billion yen (about $5.9 billion U.S.) over the previous year's total of ¥412.3 billion yen for the same period.

This phenomenon is not limited to little children and teenagers. Ninety-three percent of people who make the actual purchase of computer games and 83 percent of people who make the actual purchase of video games age 18 or older. There is a solid adult following that fuels this financial juggernaut. I also told my seatmate that I wasn't kidding when I use the term "juggernaut." Videogame sales worldwide will rival or overtake those of several major corporations.

Data shows that this pop culture icon is now a mainstream item and has made huge inroads into our society. The average age of video game players is over 30. In 2005, 25 percent of gamers were over the age of 50. I turned to her with a big smile and said, "I know that this is true because I am one of them." Furthermore, an interesting trend that is growing is that women age 18 or older represent an increasingly greater portion of the game-playing population.

Adult gamers have been playing video games for an average of 12 years. Fifty-three percent of today's game players expect to be playing as much, or more 10 years from now. Ninety-four percent of adolescents expend significant amounts of time playing video games. Males play approximately 15 hours a week and girls average 10 to 12 hours per week.

Video games impact even the youngest of age groups. Preschoolers between the ages of two and five play video games an average of 28 minutes per day. This is going to aggressively increase, as devices get more powerful and portable, with more intuitive interfaces.

The prevalence and access to video games has truly penetrated every venue of society. A study of over 2,000 eight to 18-year-olds (3rd through 12th graders) found that 83 percent of them have at least one video game player in their home, 31 percent have three or more video game players in their home, and 49 percent have video game players in their bedrooms. 95 percent of the teens surveyed said they had access to either a video game console/device or home computer, and a similar proportion (90 percent) said they owned at least one video game. Forty-four percent of most frequent video game players say they play games online, up from 19 percent in 2000. With the increased availability of broadband, this trend will continue into the future. Today, 32 percent of "heads of households" report playing video games on wireless devices such as cell phones or PDA's, up from 20 percent in 2002.

Surprisingly and contrary to popular belief, video game play has become a domestic activity with the majority of youths playing at home (46 percent of respondents) or at a friend's house (25 percent). In comparison, only 17 percent said they played at an arcade. This is a big shift from the early days when the arcade was the center of activity.

In spite of the aggressive condemnation and bad press associated with video game play, 61 percent of parents with children under the age of 18 say that computer and video games are a positive addition to their children's lives. The majority of teenagers (over 80 percent) say that playing them produced a pleasant, exciting, challenging and interesting experience. Also, contrary to popular belief, the video gamers are not flocking in hordes to blood and guts video titles. In 2005, only 30.1 percent of video games sold were action video games.

I then pointed out other facts to my opponent revealed by the data. Seventy-nine percent of video game players report exercising or playing sports an average of 20 hours per month. Ninety-three percent of video game players report reading books or daily newspapers on a regular basis. This flies in the face of some claims that video games are the major cause of intellectual deletion. But the most intriguing data, I told her, comes from research on video games and violence.

There is an increasing amount of scientific data emerging, which contradicts some of the early negative claims. According to University of Southern California sociologist Karen Sternheimer, who completed a study involving analysis of newspaper coverage and FBI statistics that detailed trends of youth crime, in the 10 years after the release of *Doom*— and many other violent video game titles—juvenile homicide arrest rates in the United States fell 77 percent. We should be very cautious when pointing to complex tragedies like Columbine and Virginia Tech and blame these heinous acts on playing violent video games.

Research in many arenas supports the presence of the positive attributes of video games. Neda Gould and colleagues at the U.S. National Institute of Mental Health in Bethesda, Maryland believe video games can even help doctors diagnose depression. In that study, the researchers used an over-the-counter title and video game console and asked participants to find their way to as many landmarks as possible within a set period of time. Depressed people found their way to an average of 2.4 landmarks, while the healthy control group found an average of 3.8 landmarks.

Sony PlayStation commissioned a study on 13 and 14-year-olds by psychologist Dr. David Lewis. He found that participants retained over three-quarters of the facts presented to them in a historical video game as opposed to retention of just more than half by those who were presented with the same information in written form. *MediEvil 2*, a game set in Victorian times was used to test the children.

Finally, I told my seatmate about my own study, which revealed that surgeons who had played video games in the past for more than three hours per week, made 37 percent fewer errors, were 27 percent faster, and scored 42 percent better overall in a surgical skill program than surgeons who never played video games.

After this unrelenting onslaught of facts, it was apparent that this young lady was literally shell shocked. She had that look puppies get after doing something they should not have done. The initial confidence in her original position began melting like butter on a hot grill. The only response she could utter was, "Gosh, I didn't know that." That is when I decided to go in for the kill, assassinate her argument once and for all, and bring her over from the dark side.

My next step was to give my personal testimony on how pop culture and video games had impacted my life. Besides, it was time to put this debate to an end. We were going to be landing soon and I didn't want this contest to end in a "no decision."

The Knockout Blow: Me, My Life and Video Games

I began by telling her about my life and how it has been greatly influenced by video games and other pop culture icons. Growing up in the segregated Mississippi Delta, television offered a peep into a world beyond the plantation. The shows that most impacted my life were Looney Tunes cartoons, *Gun Smoke*, *Ben Casey, M.D.*, *The Jetsons*, and *Star Trek*. To the causal observer, cartoons are only a source of entertainment. But, old school cartoons like the Looney Tunes series gave me more than comedic relief. It supplied initial exposure to historical events, famous personalities, and exposure to the possibilities of space travel. The adventures and antics of Bugs Bunny, Elmer Fudd, Daffy Duck, Yosemite Sam and their other buddies were an oasis of much needed exposure to the past, present and future of our society.

I know that these cartoons have been ridiculed as being senseless and violent, but remember; you cannot judge a book by its cover. Believe it or not, the cartoons were the source of my first exposure to classical music. On the playground, I would hum such scores as the "Blue Danube," and Beethoven's Fifth Symphony. My friends were amazed at how well I could name these gems of classical music while we watched *Jeopardy*. My exposure to classical music by watching Looney Tunes cartoons gave me an appreciation of this musical genre that I would never have been able to cultivate otherwise.

Gun Smoke was another television program that greatly influenced my life. From that show, I developed an appreciation of our country's formative years as we struggled to mature as a nation. The adventurous spirit of the settlers of the Wild West was very encouraging, and I could identify with them as they struggled on the new frontier, and as I grew up in the South in the 1960s. All my life, it seems as if I have been a designated pioneer, the first or one of the first. I was in college at 16. I was one of only a few blacks who had attended the University of Mississippi at the time; yes, the same University of Mississippi that experienced days of riots when James Meredith, a black man, dared to integrate the institution

100 years after the Civil War was fought. I was the third black to graduate from the institution and go on to its medical school.

Not only did *Gun Smoke* show me the benefits of rugged individualism, it also taught me good manners. I admired the way that Marshall Dillon would tip his hat to a lady and how he would artfully avoid a confrontation by establishing his authority without being offensive, unless he had no other choice. From watching him, I developed a sense of responsibility to come to the aid of the downtrodden. I want to stress that first and foremost, I had great parents and a cohesive community to support me, but this show served as one of the beacons in my life that helped shape my responsible entry into manhood.

As I continued, I told my seatmate, I would not be where I am now if it weren't for the show *Ben Casey, M.D.* This guy, a neurosurgeon, was my hero, even though most of his patients died. Vince Edward's portrayal of this character with his matter of fact, callous exterior was awesome. Dr. House had nothing on him. He carried the role of the hard, no nonsense physician while subtly flashing a glimpse of a vulnerable and soft underbelly. Now that takes range. I loved the way, on numerous occasions, he took on potentially confidence-eradicating odds of failure (the patient dying) and attacked the situation with a self-assured tenacity. And when he had a patient who survived, it wiped out the memory of all the other tragedies. Because of Dr. Casey, I was convinced at an early age to become a healer and my fate was sealed to become a surgeon.

Television, as I continue to tell my story, even had something to do with my love for science and technology. The show that opened my eyes to the potential of technology was *The Jetsons*. Interplanetary space travel, flying cars, mobile audio and video communications, remotely controlled appliances and robots, were all stimulating concepts of the landscape of the future presented in that show. For those familiar with the program, close your eyes and try to conjure up the image of Elroy Jetson's room. Can you see his desk? Now, can you remember when his mother would talk to him from another part of the house, or his father would call him from work?

All of this was conducted from a television-like device. But he never used it to watch television shows. Most often, he could be found using this device to perform homework or general communication with others including his robotic teacher. This was the 1960's and this represented my first exposure to the concept of a personal computer. For me it was a revelation, this futuristic device was more than a lifestyle enhancement item for Elroy; it helped to explain why he was able to have the knowledge and awareness of a Ph.D. in physics and he was only 10-years-old.

The breadth and scope of his life was expanded by this miracle of technology. It left me hungering for any material on technological advancement that would allow me to gain insight into Elroy's world that I hoped one day would be mine.

But these shows pale in comparison to the show that became a treasure chest of inspiration for me, the groundbreaking *Star Trek* series. It had what I call the triple threat of beyond-the-horizon-societal evolutionary material. The show featured out-of-this-world technology, the boundless adventure of the exploration of space, and the prospect of societal evolution. The seemingly perpetual in-your-face demonstration of miracles of the future jumped out and grabbed viewers with each episode. The thought of a transporter device capable of displacing molecules of organic matter to a predetermined geographic point and back again, put my mind into sensory overload. Even more amazing was the fact that in spite of this chaos of molecular dismemberment, the chief engineer, Mr. Scott, and even ensign Johnson were able to reassemble their passengers—or were they victims—without them assuming the configuration of a salamander.

The picture of Captain Kirk standing on the bridge looking out into the vastness of space and confidently uttering the word, "Engage," touched something deep within my soul. This show said to me there was hope for me touch the American dream despite the social inequities of the day. On *Star Trek*, I saw for the first time diverse races of people working together without conflict and with a startling oneness. This show presented a visual representation of the unification of the human race that could one day be achieved.

I just had to concentrate my efforts on being prepared to participate in the revolution of change that I strongly felt was going to come in my life time. This asset transcended the show's entertainment value. It showed what society could be if we decided that we would not be our worst enemies. If we interacted with each other, with fairness and without the contamination of inaccurate perceptions, what a beautiful world this could be.

For me, the societal evolution portrayed in this show was essential to the shaping of my future. During my years growing up in the Jim Crow South, the prevailing policy was that the races should live in separate but equal strata of society. I could not go to the same amusement parks. I could not receive a meal at the same venue in the Kentucky Fried Chicken or go to the same school as white children. Outside of my parents, there were minimal role models for me in areas other than the profession of driving a tractor or digging a ditch. I grew up during a painful period of this country's history where the misguided policies of a few were allowed to stain the souls of the masses.

It was very tempting for me during those formative years to develop a hatred toward those that would commit atrocities of violence toward fellow members of the human race just because of their skin color. The positive images of serenity portrayed in the midst of diversity displayed on *Star Trek* helped me to suppress the development of the destructive momentum of hate. White people were not the enemy. Hate was the common enemy to us all. Hate imprisons the spirit and causes the dissolution of hope. Hate makes you like those who seek to oppress.

This visionary show, along with the teachings of my faith and guidance of my parents and immediate family, helped me to grow up free of hatred toward those that would see me as being less than a man. Finally, this show helped me place my mindset into a continuous search mode with a key component being the never-ending quest for knowledge. Acquisition of knowledge is the fuel of fantasy that leads to the production of dreams, which is the mother of all inspiration and innovation.

On the brink of becoming emotional, I stopped to take a breath at this point. As I looked into the face of the young lady, I could see that her transformation was all but complete. I gathered myself and continued my story by telling her that while television had a huge impact in my early development and prepared me for adolescence and adulthood in so many ways; it also paved the way for a lifelong appreciation and affiliation with video games.

For me, video games represented a new form of freedom, the freedom of exploration and individual expression. It allowed me to try things without the fear of penalty with the perpetual presence of competition and reward. It also provided a reservoir of entertainment that eased the monotony of endless hours of academic study. It allowed me to maintain contact with the spirit of a terminal 12-year-old that continues today to fuel my relentless drive for achievement and contribution to society.

From the influence of *Pong* that helped me get an 'A' in tennis class, to *Asteroids* which allowed me to experience first hand the consequences of principles of physics such as gravitational pull and momentum, to the sanity-sustaining entertainment provided by *Donkey Kong*, video games have been a constant companion at the heart of what makes Butch Rosser, Butch Rosser. Whatever the public perception of my contribution to society, it is steadfastly entwined with the presence and evolution of video games in my life.

I will never forget my first encounter with video games. It was the early 1970s and I was a sophomore in college. I was tired of studying and I went to the student union to see if any of my friends were there. As I was walking toward the game area, I noticed this synthetic blipping sound coming from the general area where the pinball machines were located. The sound seemed very familiar. It sounded as if there was a ping-pong table in the room, but the mystery deepened because there was not enough space for any ping-pong tables in there. Then I heard it, my favorite past time, trash talkin'. I don't care if it is a baby diaper changing competition or a game of jacks, you knew where the fun was if you heard trash talkin'.

High-level competition and trash talkin' go together like white on rice. I hurried to the room to see what had inspired such a spirited assembly. Lo and behold, to my surprise, I did find a game of ping-pong, but it was not being played on a table. It was being played on a television screen. There was a virtual net, a ball, paddles and more importantly, tons of fun. I quickly got in line to get my shot at the current champ. After I had been playing for about an hour, I asked the guys the name of this game. They told me that it was a new thing called a video game and the name of the game was *Pong*.

On that day, I discovered a new outlet that would always be there to comfort me while I wrestled with typical college student feelings of underachievement, extreme course loads, and social challenges with friends and other students. Instead of drugs, I funneled my recreational energy into video games and it would be a move I would not regret. I needed this outlet for decompression because I was not your typical college student. As I mentioned before, I entered college at age 16, a time when most of my childhood friends were still high school sophomores. This would present a daunting situation for even the most mature of children. It would have been quite easy to succumb to the pressure.

But my parents and grandparents were mainstays of stability throughout all of this. In spite of my arguments to the contrary, my parents did not think much about video games. They did not want to support anything that would take me away from my studies. But, come to think about it, my Dad did not want me to go to the movies because it wasted too much time. You do the math on that one.

Thank God for my grandparents! They understood what I was going through and the age-inappropriate amount of pressure I was under. The way they viewed it, anything constructive that was going to help me deal with the challenges I was facing was a good thing. My grandparents helped to support my love affair with video games by buying me one of the first *Pong* home consoles. I am grateful my parents purposefully looked the other way. Thank God for every little miracle!

In spite of all my challenges during my undergraduate years, I was blessed to make the cut and be admitted into medical school. This was my dream come true. I was only 20-years-old when I began the most rigorous academic test of my life. I also had the added responsibility of being a husband, and soon thereafter, a father; I never did things the easy way. On October 6, 1975, I was blessed with my first child, Kevin Sidney Rosser. A second child, Duane Charles Rosser came in 1977, and my first daughter, Angela Nicole Rosser followed in 1980. There were those of the opinion that no one in their right mind would knowingly have children so early with the tremendous pressures that I carried, but it was okay with me.

In spite of the very serious posture of my circumstances, video games still took a labored step forward in my life. I had always dreamed of having enough kids to have a family baseball team. But, as reality set in, I made an adjustment to my original plan. It was not easy, but having kids early dictated a situation where we all had to grow up together. As we grew, we discovered that we shared a large amount of common ground. We all loved amusement parks, movies and music. We also shared a love for video games. This is a common ground we still share today. My early entrance into fatherhood ensured that the influence of video games would not be like an old soldier that fades away; rather, video games would continue to serve as a testimony to my permanent encasement in the perpetually hopeful mindset of a child's youthful enthusiasm.

On October 17, 1996, I got two new additions to the Rosser video game guild with the birth of Taylor Elyse and Tianna Marie Rosser. They were twin bundles of joy and were more partners to play out the saga of my video game odyssey. On December 7, 2005, my first grandchild, Easton, was born. With his arrival, I saw no end in sight for my fun. This brought a chuckle and a smile for my long-exhausted debate adversary.

In 1980, I was finishing my senior year in medical school and I was really cruising. This was my final year, and I was in a comfort zone. I was on the hospital wards taking care of people. This is the thing that I had always wanted to do. Finally all that book learning could be used for something more than regurgitating facts on a test. Applying what I had learned to take care of people quickly became intuitive, which allowed me to re-engage in more recreational efforts. Of course that meant re-exploring my love of video games. Boy, a lot had happened since my grandparents bought that home *Pong* console.

Lunar Lander, *Pacman*, and *Asteroids* had just come onto the scene. *Lunar Lander* and *Asteroids* cultivated the *Star Trek* seed in me that had been planted so long ago. The making of *Star Wars* further heightened my appreciation of space video games. In fact, the day after I graduated from medical school, my friend, Charles King and I went to the arcade and played all those games for hours. It was my graduation gift to myself. At this great moment in my life, I was Luke Skywalker and the Force was with me. What a great time to be alive. And then the dark side descended upon my world once again—surgical residency.

Even though I anticipated giving up video games during this time, I loved being a surgical resident. Walking the halls of the hospital with my white coat and scrubs, treating gunshot wounds in the emergency room, orchestrating the stabilization of a patient in the intensive care unit, or coming to the aid of a patient who had suddenly experienced a turn for the worse were things I looked forward to everyday.

Like my hero Ben Casey, I was my happiest in the operating room, on center stage performing a delicate ballet between skill and art to intervene on a patient's behalf with my surgical expertise. Like fighter pilots, surgeons always live with death a whisper away, therefore, we work hard and we play hard. In spite of my fear that video games would be extinguished from my life, I managed to make sure that I played a lot of video games.

Everyone knew that the surgery residents rocked! Tom Diehl, Jan Elston and I were the ringleaders. We were the first to get the Intellivision home console and we hooked it up in the residents' on-call quarters. No one could watch *Saint Elsewhere* when we were getting our Intellivision groove on. Battles of mythical proportions with Intellibaseball, football and golf were commonplace. There were times when we had crowds cheering for their favorite players. Heck, they may as well; we had the game connected to the only TV in the joint.

In July of 1984, Tom Diehl and I became chief residents of surgery, and we pledged an oath to Jan Elston, the outgoing chief, that we would maintain our tradition of fun and video game heritage.

During this time, my children were growing up and they were great fun. I would often embrace them with one great big bear hug and say, "I love you guys! You are the best! If you were not mine, I would rent you!" I said that then and I still feel that way today. And they all loved to play video games with their Dad. They did not get tired of playing, even though they did grow impatient with Daddy winning all the time. I was happier than a pig in slop because I had some video gaming buddies who also thought that I was the coolest Dad on the planet.

By the fall of 1990, there was a huge leap forward in medical technology. Cameras had now become very small and produced brilliant high-resolution digital images. This would provide the foundation for one of the most monumental strides ever taken in the history of surgery. The tiny camera equipment was combined with small telescopes and surgeons could now go on a fantastic voyage through the body without opening the patient up with a large incision. The approach was called laparoscopic, or keyhole surgery. With laparoscopic surgery, the images of the patient's anatomy could be presented on a television screen.

The surgeon could insert long, thin instruments into the patient's abdomen and then manipulate them like joysticks. These instruments are used to perform surgical procedures like the removal of a gallbladder or appendix while the surgeon looks up at a television monitor to help guide his/her every move. It really is ironic, I told my rapt listener, that the craft for which I had trained for so long was now more like the video games that I had played for fun. Talk about the best of both worlds.

This fusion of my world of work with my world of play was associated with my big professional breakthrough in December 1990. Dr. Herbert Awender and I embarked on the exploration of a new high tech surgical frontier when we performed the first gallbladder removal using this new technique at Akron General Medical Center in Akron, Ohio. Unlike many of the horror stories that we had heard about with this surgery at other institutions, we sailed through our first procedure in one and a half hours.

During that first operation, my skill level allowed me to feel totally in my element. I made tactical and technique adjustments intuitively. After the case was over, in the presence of the staff and countless onlookers, an industry representative commented, "Hey Butch, you look as if you have done a thousand of these." I quickly replied, "It's because of all the video games I play." I looked over at Dr. Awender and gave him a wink and a smile. He smiled and winked back. He knew that a star had been born that he had helped to create, and I was about to fly on my own and fly very high. For as long as I live, I will always remember the day I used this approach for the first time. I felt like Captain Kirk taking the bridge of the Starship Enterprise and uttering the immortal words, "Mr. Sulu, engage!"

"Wow," was the only word that my former opponent could utter. I took advantage of the silence that followed, and for the last few minutes of our flight I tried to make some final strategic points. I presented them in rapid sequence like the end of a firework show. I began by telling her that, contrary to popular belief, video games were originally created by some of the most brilliant minds that our nation had to offer. Video games are not the result of an entrepreneurial orgy of greed designed to bring profit at the expense of the slaughter of this nation's youth. The video game phenomenon is literally everywhere and embraced by many. I closed my argument by asking her to forgive me for acting upon my desire to harness, with scientific due diligence, this tremendous resource for the greater good.

As if on cue, the end of our conversation was punctuated by the familiar double dong, which signaled that we had arrived at our destination. It was time for us to gather our things and go. My opponent was now my friend and to my surprise, my ranting had touched this young lady of noble intentions. But it had bigger implications. This chance meeting on an airplane ride had put me in a position to give a sermon that I had never given before. I had exposed my passion and commitment to the cause of capturing the best qualities that video games have to offer. I had spent the last two hours presenting the data and making the case for mounting a full investigative effort committed to the study of video games.

The immediate effect was that I had inoculated this learned scholar, with impeccable academic credentials from an institution of unquestioned heritage, with a virus that infected her with a commitment to the cause and a revolution. On that airplane, on that day, she decided that she would build her legacy on the study of the power of video games to empower teachers to touch a generation that could save a nation. The larger effect: my life was touched in a special way because then and there, I decided that I would become dedicated to spreading the word like I had just done on that plane. While my opponent may have lost the debate, society won a warrior for the greater good. And my hope is that we all can win!

CHAPTER THREE
THE CHRONICLES OF THE X BOX DOC

The great plane-ride debate happened in 2005. While that exchange galvanized my commitment to my current course, the spark that really began the journey to write this book occurred very innocently many years before. I told you the short version of the story in the previous chapter. Please indulge me as I give you the longer version.

In 1990, when I was a young assistant professor and attending surgeon at Akron General Medical Center and Northeastern Ohio College of Medicine in Akron, Ohio, the word of my prowess at performing laparoscopic surgery rapidly spread around the world. Subsequently, the Learning Channel produced a documentary featuring me removing a gallbladder using this amazing technique. I was then featured on the "Miracle Child Telethon," which featured my removal of the gallbladder of one of the youngest patients at the time, a 17-month-old boy. This new type of surgery was proving to be a modern day miracle. Patients could have major surgery and afterward appear to have just gone for a walk in the park. Many began calling it "band aid" surgery because the only evidence that a procedure had been done ware the band-aids used to cover the four one-half-inch incisions. Visitors from around the world began coming to watch my technique.

On one occasion, three surgeons visited from Germany. This was a very special day, because I was going to remove an appendix that was about to rupture and all of the work was to be done through four small incisions less than a half-inch in size. At the time, this was a rarely-performed operation because of the requirement of a very advanced surgical skill set. Also in the operating room that day was a young female reporter who was there to cover the story about my international guests.

Everyone watched in amazement as I looked at the TV monitor and delicately moved the handles of my long, thin instruments to isolate and disconnect the appendix from the right side of the large intestine. At this point, one of the surgeons who had been very negative and skeptical, pounced with a booming voice and said, "Now, what are you going to do with the remaining stump of the appendix? You must bury it in the tissues to prevent infection. You have to place a surgical suture to do that and we all know that this cannot be done with this new technique."

I promptly placed a needle and suture into the abdomen and in under a minute I had done that which he said was impossible. Under my mask, I smiled because I saw my visitors in speechless awe of what they had just witnessed. Without a word being uttered, without any fanfare, I placed the appendix into a specimen bag and removed it through the patient's belly button. The infected area was washed with salt solution and the incisions were closed with the stitches, all under the skin. The incisions were barely visible and the entire operation was performed in less than 30 minutes.

Less than 12 hours later, I made rounds with my new friends. As we were getting off the elevator, there was my patient, walking without pain, smiling and hungry. I wrote orders that allowed her to eat and she went home six hours later. With the old technique, patients undergoing an appendectomy had a hospital stay of two to seven days, with a one to two month recovery period. This patient had been admitted, operated on and then discharged in 18 hours. She went back to work in a week.

The surgeons were very excited, and so was the reporter. She wrote an article about the experience, and I will never forget one of her opening remarks. "I had the privilege of seeing the future of surgery. I saw an appendix removed by Dr. Butch Rosser, the Nintendo Surgeon." I remember how struck I was by her comments. What did she mean by the Nintendo surgeon? And then it hit me. From her vantage point, she saw a surgeon sitting down at an operating table about to operate on a patient. She looked at my hands and saw me moving two instrument handles rising out of the abdomen, much like joysticks. And then she saw my eyes peering with fierce fixation on the activity on a television screen. Then I got it! The image I just described was that of someone playing a video game. Could it be that my seemingly intuitive skill in this new surgical environment was because of my years of video game play? Could it be that what I had always played for fun could now be the key to my success as a surgeon? Sweeeeeeeet!! This event would change the course of my life and is directly tied to my writing this book.

In the beginning, it left me with a mixed bag of emotions. I was happy that I was helping my patients by practicing this modern day miracle of medicine. I was proud that others around the world had interest in my techniques. I was flattered that the lay media thought this to be noteworthy enough to present to the public, but I was faced with multiple unsettling dilemmas.

I was sad because I knew that all patients did not have this service available to them due to the dearth of skilled surgeons offering these procedures. Only about 10 percent of the surgeons around the world could offer this type of advanced procedure at the time. I was also sad because I knew there was a steep learning curve involved in gaining the skill needed to be safe and competent. For instance, one of the most basic of surgical tasks— suturing and knot tying—took over 300 hours to learn how to do laparoscopically.

Something as simple as tying a knot is not as easy as it seems in this kind of surgery. Imagine tying your shoelaces using three-foot-long chopsticks while not directly looking at your shoes and having only the image on a television screen to guide you. These challenges were not what you would call low hanging fruit. There was no way the special educational needs of this fledgling surgical art form were going to be addressed with less than an "outside of the box" effort. So I decided to dedicate myself to spreading the miracle of laparoscopic surgery around the world through education.

This would be no small task, but the journey to the solution of all big problems starts with the first little step. My first little step would be designing a training program that could teach other surgeons how to suture laparoscopically in 12 hours rather than over 300. Okay, I had jumped out of the airplane. Now the question was whether I had a parachute that would open? I was left alone to answer the haunting question, "How am I going to do all this? Interestingly, I would combine the loves of my life to get it done, football, aviation and video games.

My football background would prove important because of the training techniques that I was exposed to. Difficult skills and tasks were deconstructed into easier mini-tasks that had increasing degrees of difficulty. These were learned and practiced first. Competency in the preparatory drills led to mastery of more difficulty tasks. I used a similar approach to laparoscopic suturing, which is the most difficult task in surgery. I went around the world to videotape great master surgeons who could suture but did not have an organized approach to training others. After countless hours of reviewing tapes, just like a football coach, I charted the number of steps and technique tendencies. This helped me to come up with the most efficient sequence of events. The resulting procedural flow was a blend of several techniques including my own. In the next step, I had to validate or prove that the technique flow I suggested, and the preparatory drills needed to help a student get up to speed were indeed reliable in producing consistently good results. I first identified 10 mini-tasks that I felt had features of skills needed to perform the suturing sequence. At the time, I had no way of knowing if these tasks had any valid correlation with suturing.

I therefore began a series of investigations to identify which of these preparatory drills had a scientific link with surgeons learning how to suture. As I mentioned before, I began with 10, but only three showed scientific correlation. This would prove to be a great help in shortening the time required to train because we did not have to complete unhelpful exercises.

The next step was to determine the proper flow and set-up of the course. My inspiration came from the aviation field. I have had a love affair with aviation since I was a little boy in Moorhead, Mississippi lying on my back watching crop dusters going about their aerial ballet in order to protect crops and help them grow. At age five, I was a walking encyclopedia filled with knowledge about airplanes, aviation and its history. After much study, I found that there were many similarities between the early days of laparoscopic surgery and the early days of aviation.

In the early days of aviation, the accident rates for aircrafts operating in bad weather and at night were unacceptably high, as aviation pioneers sought to stretch the edge of the envelope. This profile of poor outcomes, if not corrected, would serve to impede the growth of the fledgling aviation industry. We were seeing similar issues with laparoscopic surgery. In the beginning, there were many patient injuries because surgeons without training and guidance tried to perform the surgery.

In aviation, the "fix" to their problem came in the form of a campaign, led by Jimmy Doolittle and others, for the development and use of simulators to prepare pilots for adverse conditions by practicing under realistic conditions ahead of time. Simulators in aviation training became a reality, and in two years, the accident rate in bad weather and at night decreased by 90 percent. The impact of simulation training and aircrew team building has continued to help the aerospace industry to proliferate while maintaining an outstanding safety record. I believed that we could follow a similar path in laparoscopic surgery. I would apply the same lesson learned from aviation to produce a simulator-based training program for surgeons.

In addition to a customized simulator program, I drew on another piece of aviation history that involved the military's response to sub-par performance with dogfight engagements in the early days of the Vietnam conflict. Our Air Force had a disappointing kill ratio of 2:1. At the end of World War II and the Korean Conflict it was 10-12:1. The Navy aggressively sought to identify and correct deficiencies responsible for the poor performance.

They surmised that their current training paradigm was flawed. There was not enough training time, the training time was not properly structured, and it did not have metrics to measure and evaluate performance. A total revamping of fighter weapons tactics training would have to be undertaken. The special school that served as the home of this new training philosophy was called Top Gun.

Top Gun was a six-week long training experience for fighter pilots that pushed the aircrews and equipment beyond their previously believed capabilities and made them better. It stressed the fundamentals of air combat maneuvering. It served to facilitate the "standardization of excellence" by defining the indefinable element of what makes a good fighter pilot. This was achieved by establishing measuring units that guided a validated structured training sequence. These pilots, the "best of the best," were then re-deployed to the fleet to train other members of their squadrons. The program paid immediate results and by the end of the Vietnam Conflict, the Navy's kill ratio increased to 12:1.

On the other hand, the U.S. Air Force did not readily adopt such a program and its kill ratio only increased to 3:1. Later, they saw the light and today show a similar record of excellence. The legacy of this bold initiative continues today. Since that time, no American aircraft has been lost during aerial combat—truly an astounding record.

The *Top Gun* movie had an important impact on pop culture's perception of what is cool. Tom Cruise, with his "Maverick" call sign and to-the-wall attitude, riding his motorcycle with the leather flight jacket, listening to great music and getting the girl, is a pop culture icon of landmark proportions.

I used all of the above to construct a unique program that, if followed, would teach surgeons—no matter what age or experience—to perform laparoscopic suturing after 12 hours of training. The course was dubbed the

"Top Gun Laparoscopic Skills and Suturing Program." It proudly patterns itself after the training methodology that formed the core curriculum of the Navy's Top Gun school for fighter pilots. This includes a deconstruction of complex tasks to their most elemental level, the execution of preparatory drills to facilitate complex task execution, team building, and the use of metrics to objectively evaluate performance. The course is also very cost effective because it can be done without animal models, and by using low cost tabletop simulators.

But another colossal challenge that I still had to face was how would I get surgeons, who can be legends in their own minds, to humble themselves and willingly participate in something that forces them to first admit that they have performance deficiencies? In my first published paper on the subject, it was discovered that only 18 percent of self-proclaimed advanced laparoscopic surgeons could tie a surgical knot laparoscopically in 10 minutes. That is a lifetime in surgery; someone else's lifetime. A patient could bleed to death if you cannot tie off a bleeding blood vessel.

To meet this challenge I used my experience with video games. I designed the program around the methods and techniques that video game developers use to hook players the first time they play a game.

Surgeons and fighter pilots are some of the most competitive personalities on the planet. My plan was to tap into the competitive nature that drives them to be successful no matter what the cost. From my video game experience, I knew that there was a need to have a score associated with performance of each task. Once there is a score, it serves as a jockey to make these thoroughbreds give maximum effort each time out and like it. In my course, the scores are based on the time required to complete the task under the rigorous direction of the Top Gun instructors.

In addition, each time your instrument strays inappropriately outside the performance envelope, a bright red light comes on, a buzzer sounds loudly, and an error is counted. If this sounds familiar, it should, because this is the same format of the "Operation" board game. Each time you commit an error, your score has to absorb a five second penalty. So the participants have to be fast, but accurate. This is an important trait to have as a surgeon. As in golf, the lower the score, the better you are. All the scores are placed into a database. Today that database is made up of over 5,000 surgeons. Surgeons are now able to have a report card that shows their percentile ranking compared to their peers.

The student scores are dynamically displayed to the entire group throughout the course. Similar to a squadron-ready room aboard an aircraft carrier, the leader board at a golf tournament, and to your favorite video game title, you are what your score says you are, and you are what you are until you beat that score. The opportunity to achieve and display a score is the breeding ground of competition, and in my opinion competition is the mother of excellence.

In addition, demonstrations of superior expertise were strategically placed during the course to show the students there was always another level they had to try to reach. One of the most entertaining elements involves me tying a suture standing on one leg with my non-dominant hand, while having my dominant eye blindfolded. Invariably, even with these restrictions, my score is far superior to the best student in the group. When I complete my run, I customarily turn triumphantly to the group and thump my chest and declare, "Who's yo' Daddy now?! Ladies and gentlemen, if you do not have a better score, you were just beat by a peg leg, one armed, blind man!"

For a moment you can hear a pin drop in the lab. Then there is a stampede back to the tables to try to beat what they just saw. Of course my demonstration has no application to a real surgery but it definitely serves as motivation to drive the students to be the best they can be.

During the course, there is an ever-present possibility of winning and reward. Awards of distinction are given to participants who have competed with superior skill at the end of the course. First through third place awards are presented to the best of the best in multiple categories.

In addition, awards are given for the Most Valuable and Most Improved participant. The participant with the average of the lowest score in all categories is crowned Top Gun. The winner receives a huge trophy and a leather flight jacket and an open invitation to go anywhere in the world to help conduct courses as a Top Gun instructor.

The ferocity of the competition is amazing. But it is all of the collaborative variety within the framework of team play. The course is designed to have a large group separated into small teams that have the common challenge of finishing all of the exercises in the required time. If teamwork and focus is not practiced at all times, the entire group could fail. This serves as an example of "collaborative competition" where there is a common goal and everyone is competing to get there. I will speak to this later when we talk about the collateral learning assets of video games.

Great surgeons are not born; rather, they are made by a commitment and willingness to pay the price for excellence. This unique course cast from the signature of football, aviation, and video games served to not only facilitate development of surgical skills, but mastery of the most difficult task that has to be executed in the surgical world, laparoscopic suturing. Subsequently, the program has been shown to be effective in training surgical residents and even medical and college students with no surgical training.

I did not have long to celebrate this achievement because I had built a Ferrari that nobody wanted to drive. Many leading American surgeons thought that I was a heretic. I could not find support for my course in this country. Even though my current issues had nothing to do with race, I used a strategy followed by many people of color at the start of last century. I turned to a more open-minded Europe to see if my program could get a fair look. As a result, the first Top Gun Laparoscopic Skill and Suturing Program was held in 1992 on the island of Aruba, a Dutch holding, sponsored by the Academic Medical Center in Amsterdam, Holland.

Joris Bannenberg and Dirk Meijer, M.D./Ph.D. research assistants in the department of surgery, were in charge of organizing and executing training programs for laparoscopic gallbladder removal. Both embraced the highly structured and entertaining educational format I developed for suturing.

The first course was a great success and included 20 participants from eight countries. None of the participants could tie a knot within 10 minutes at the beginning of the course; however, all could perform the task in less than two minutes at the end of the course. After the first course, the popularity of the program spread like wildfire. Just like that, the concept tipped and it has continued to gain momentum ever since. It has been featured all over the world and showcased in the media. Over 50 institutions around the world have adopted the program in some form since its inception and four of the most prestigious surgical societies have featured the program.

One would think I would have been happy with my accomplishments, but I wasn't. I was still challenged by a question that had followed me since the day I removed that appendix and read the comments about my exploits by a young reporter. Were video games the source of my intuitiveness in this world of surgical screens? If they were, could I scientifically identify which ones are the best ones to play? And could I seamlessly integrate video game play into our Top Gun surgical curriculum and enhance the program's already legendary effectiveness?

To address these questions, I designed a research project and gathered scientific evidence. The research was done over three years, and the paper, "The Impact of Video Games in Surgical Training," was published in February 2007 in the *Archives of Surgery*. The following is a summary of those findings:

Thirty-three resident and attending physicians participating in the Top Gun Skills Acquisition Course offered at Beth Israel Medical Center between 2001 and 2003 were recruited to participate in this study. The primary outcome measures were correlations between participants' laparoscopic suturing skills, video game scores and video game experience. The participants filled out a questionnaire to assess video game play. It included questions pertaining to episodes of play, length of time playing, types of games played and familiarity with specific genres of games. The participants were then allowed to take part in the video game exercises. Three games were selected out of over 200 that were screened. Each game was chosen based on its applicability to the development of specific skills required for completion of the Top Gun Laparoscopic Skills and Suturing Course.

The skills tested by these games included fine motor control, visual attention processing, spatial distribution, reaction time, eye-hand coordination, targeting, non-dominant hand emphasis, and 2D depth perception compensation. Three games were identified that had statistical correlation to suturing; these were: *Super Monkey Ball*, *Silent Scope* (practice mode) and *Star Wars Racer: Revenge*.

Past video gamers playing in excess of three hours per week made 37 percent fewer errors ($p < 0.02$) and performed 27 percent faster ($p < 0.03$) than their non-video game-playing colleagues. Current video gamers scored 42 percent better overall in the Top Gun Suturing Course. There was also a significant correlation between proficiency at video games and proficiency at laparoscopic surgical tasks, including suturing.

In addition, regression analyses indicated that video game skill is a significant predictor of demonstrated laparoscopic skills, after controlling for sex, years of medical training, and number of laparoscopic cases performed.

The thought of video game play being the most important factor in developing a laparoscopic surgeon's skills, was truly shocking. Thus, based on these findings, the selected video games have been made a permanent part of the Top Gun Course.

Steven Schwaitzberg, Visiting Associate Professor of Surgery at Harvard Medical School and Chief of Surgery, Cambridge Health Alliance, has strong opinions as to how video games fit into the learning paradigm of surgeons and physicians:

Children are going to play video games. Can we turn this into something useful? Much of modern surgery is done on a video screen using chopstick-like instruments or even robotic controls. We know that young surgeons have a wide variety of skill levels even before they place their first suture. Did their upbringing influence these differences? If great musicians and athletes are trained from an early age, what about your surgeon?

My point is why aren't we teasing out those aspects of the virtual video game environment that could equip our future generations to do some good? What skills do airline pilots need? Shouldn't we figure out if there are talents that can be nurtured for careers like flying? The cockpit is a complex environment. A lot of things are happening at once. Can we equip future generations of pilots by subtly modifying the gaming choices of their youth to better handle their future needs?

Because the media constantly surrounds our children, we ought to ensure they get something useful out of it. We should explore strategy games that our future generals should be playing in addition to great games like chess to enhance their strategic abilities. You might suppose this sounds a bit far-fetched, but it reminds me of a truly intriguing series of books written by Orson Scott Card, the first of which is called *Ender's Game*. I won't spoil the finale for you, but the premise is that it is not just jobs we need to prepare our children for, it is life."

The news of my findings has circled the globe multiple times. My face has been plastered all over the world, from CNN to You Tube. The program even crossed over to pop culture media when it was featured as the subject matter on an episode of the hit television show *Grey's Anatomy* in 2006. It was great seeing the senior surgeon step up and humble the resident by suturing with his eyes closed. The only thing that could have made it better was if I could have starred as myself.

Over the years, Top Gun has gained a reputation as a cutting-edge example of a blended educational program that has matured and been refined by scientific investigation and validation. The program sustains consistent outcomes that are driven by a strong dose of pop culture that includes music and video game design methodology, tactics, techniques and products. Intense scientific investigative due diligence has transformed what was a focused effort to empower surgeons to suture during laparoscopic procedures, into a skill and knowledge transfer juggernaut that has applicability to arenas beyond medicine.

Beyond the Shadow of Surgery

As usual, I could not leave well enough alone. I was compelled to see what was beyond the known performance envelope of this training and educational technique. My expedition would take me into the realm of non-medical education, K-16. I was convinced that I could package all that I had learned with my surgical experience and parlay that into general education. God knows there is immense room for improvement. For those who doubt this truth, a recent Time magazine article titled *Drop-Out Nation*, reported that three out of 10 students in the U.S. drop out of high school. This shocking statistic is even higher in some regions of the country.

Incredibly, most of these kids are not dropping out due to failing grades or poor performance; 80 percent have passing grades when they drop out. The most frequently cited reason for leaving school has been boredom, which I believe is the result of ineffective lesson plans and knowledge transfer strategies.

A solution is desperately needed if our children are to enjoy the same opportunities tomorrow as we do today. The system does not need to be destroyed, but it is in dire need of an upgrade. This overall system failure is most dramatically represented in the STEM areas: science, technology, engineering, and mathematics.

Over the past two decades, despite the enormity of the technological revolution, America's youth has failed to aggressively embrace career choices in the STEM areas. Too few students come through the K-12 system prepared or interested in these career choices. A large number of students, when given the option, avoid these and other science or high technology subjects. These factors are partly responsible for recruitment and retention problems in engineering and other technology fields.

Only 10 percent of high school graduates in the United States pursue engineering and engineering technology careers, while 20 percent of German and Japanese students pursue such careers. President Bush has placed this deficiency on a short list of high priority items that need immediate solutions because of the impact on the future of the nation.

The American Engineering Association reports that total doctoral degrees in engineering have dropped almost 10 percent since 1999 among American students, and foreign nationals now complete 57.8 percent of engineering Ph.D.s and 45.5 percent of Master's Degrees. Lack of interest in some areas of medicine has been reported. For example, 2001 was the first year that some residency spots in general surgery went unfilled. In 2007, there have been frank predictions of a doctor shortage.

Another disturbing consideration is that despite the strides made by the civil rights movement over the past 50 years in the United States, disparities in gender and racial participation in STEM areas still persists. The STEM sector is still dominated by white males. Although they constitute only 40 percent of the national work force, white males hold 69 percent of the STEM jobs, while white women (35 percent of the national work force) hold 15 percent of STEM jobs. African-Americans and Hispanics (21 percent of the national work force) hold six percent of STEM jobs, and people with disabilities (14 percent of the national work force) hold six percent of STEM jobs. In medicine, the American

Association of Medical Colleges published application and matriculation data for 2002 showing that African-Americans have a reduced acceptance rate when compared to white applicants.

Something must be done to attract women and minorities to science, technology, engineering, mathematics and medical careers. Otherwise, we will not be taking advantage of the diversity of our nation, and the innovative potential held by a large portion of our nation's work force will be lost.

I have always been concerned about this tragedy of self-exclusion practiced by today's youth, as evidenced by their lack of participation in these critical areas. Furthermore, I have always sought ways to include disenfranchised segments of society into cutting edge science- and technology-related activities.

Many would blame the children of today's generation for all of the current deficiencies. I believe that the children are not the problem, but the system is falling short. Contrary to popular belief, there are many students and individuals who have the capacity to contribute in these arenas. We need a grassroots movement to carry the message of opportunity and it needs to be told in a way that strikes a chord with people. I chose to use assets proven to capture the attention of the public, assets which will inspire, recruit and retain the public's focus. These assets are an eclectic blend of pop culture, education and fun. The vehicle I created is called the CyberSurgeon KTU (Kids-Teens-University) Program.

In spite of the medical overtures, the CyberSurgeon KTU Program is meant to promote students to be "the best they can be in no matter what they do." It seeks to attract and recruit "next gen" American innovators who will be poised to usher in a golden age of advancement, opportunity, innovation and prosperity. One focus of the program is to inspire, recruit and retain students pursuing career choices in STEM (science, technology, engineering and mathematics) and educational excellence overall. It harnesses inspiration from some of the most unlikely places: pop culture icons such as video games, cinema, television and music. In the CyberSurgeon KTU Program, this is all packaged within a competition-based environment that successfully combines learning with fun. This program defines and showcases fresh boundaries of learning that may one day find their way into the 21st century classroom.

"It's as if the National Spelling Bee met the ESPN X Games at a Jay Z rap concert," said one participant describing CyberSurgeon KTU. This program's unique 'edutainment' package also jump-starts an active door-to-door grassroots campaign that forges parental/teacher/student common ground.

Parents, after participating and seeing the impact on their children, have stated, "CyberSurgeon has given me hope; hope that with the proper balance of learning and video games, my child has a chance to be okay."

The program has several key components that draw from both educational research and from Top Gun for surgeons:

- Competition involving over-the-counter video games that have been identified by the CyberSurgeon process to be a "game for good."

- A cognitive competition featuring digital interactive "living lesson plan" curriculums in science, technology, engineering, mathematics and medicine.

- Reality-based, real world surgical simulation competitions just like in Top Gun for surgeons.

- The program uses satisfaction and performance data to maintain the program effectiveness in establishing its objectives and goals.

- Videos and music that create an environment that fuses education with entertainment to achieve "stealth learning," without sacrificing fun.

- Opportunity to compete and win, win, win all the time.

A breakthrough for the program occurred when it was featured at the Orlando Science Center annual OTRONICON event in 2006. OTRONICON is a 10-day exploration of electronic gaming and simulation that transforms the Orlando Science Center into the ultimate video gaming station. It also includes the exhibition for the latest in video games, gadgets and technology. The Orlando Science Center is one of the most state-of-the-art facilities of its kind and over 20,000 people routinely attend.

OTRONICON presents one of the hottest gaming and entertainment experiences in the Southeast. It features a video gaming tournament, platforms and accessories, workshops and product showcases, all under one roof. This event caters to everyone from kids just getting started in video gaming, to high tech professionals looking for something new, to hardcore gamers, and even—gasp!—even educators.

Dr. Brian Tonner, CEO of the center and JoAnn Neuman, the COO, gave CyberSurgeon KTU a chance at the event. It was met with overwhelming success and it was invited back in 2007. At both events, Top Gun had the place rocking with inspired learning combined with good, plain fun.

The next landmark came when Dr. Darlene Wolf was exposed to the program at OTRONICON. She is a counselor and multimedia teacher at Ocoee High School in Ocoee, Florida, a suburb of Orlando. She introduced the program to about 1,000 students at their summer school and it became another hit!

After reviewing the data, what we suspected was proven to be true. This program was not only quite attention-grabbing, but it also impacted baseline attitudes about STEM-related fields, and the students greatly appreciated it. The pre- and post-tests showed that, in the short-term, there was a statistically significant difference achieved in knowledge transfer in the subject of human anatomy. During the hour and a half program, the students' knowledge of complex anatomy soared.

The successes did not stop there. Dr. Lynn Weaver, chair of surgery at Morehouse School of Medicine in Atlanta, Georgia, introduced the program at the prestigious American College of Surgeons International Congress. Each year, hundreds of minority high school students are invited to the event and they are exposed to the world of surgery. They are divided into small groups and paired with mentors. They spend the day being exposed to the "big boys and all their toys." CyberSurgeon KTU has been a major hit of the program for the last three years.

With the aforementioned successes, momentum is building for the organization of a national tour to expose the program to more people. All of this started with visitors in my operating room 17 years ago.

Where is all of this going? I am not going to pretend that I have all of the answers. But I have seen how this program energizes people around the world. I have seen how it can impact student attitudes and accelerate learning of subject matter that many would not be interested in.

You see, I believe in the power of the average citizen. If people get it at the grassroots level, then change has a chance to happen. CyberSurgeon KTU is the nexus where technology, the scalpel, the classroom and the fulfillment of dreams, all converge on the high ground of the greater good. It showcases the power of a new learning tool (stealth learning) and builds momentum toward broader investigation and the ultimate deployment of this learning strategy into the mainstream.

Part Two

AMERiCA iN TROUBLE

● ● ● ●

This section suggests America's historical profile of global dominance can be equated to that of a sports team or corporation that has experienced a long-term winning streak or period of earning success. Similar to a sports team or corporation, a sprit of competition and a drive to win plays a very large role in our nation's success.

I then proceed to dissect this country's successful track record and identify the anatomy of traits that have made this possible. Next, an alarm is sounded to bring attention to the concern that our history of achievement and global dominance is being challenged and we are losing our position as a world leader. This erosion has been caused by the loss of our sprit of exploration, competition, and thirst for winning. All of these success-sustaining assets are being systematically deemphasized in today's society.

In order to make sure that my dissection effort doesn't turn into an autopsy, I spotlight why success and winning comes to an end. With these items identified, the case is made that video games and their unique assets can contribute to a successful turnaround of our nation. But we are going to have to be willing to *play to win*.

CHAPTER FOUR
MALAISE—YOU DON'T WANT TO HAVE IT!

As a physician, I am challenged everyday to provide answers to dilemmas that concern a patient's state of health and well-being. I am always looking for a person's chief complaint. It is what brought the patient in to see me, and it is where my efforts to heal begin.

Frequently, the chief complaint is obvious, "Doc, I was playing in a baseball game and I was hit in the chest with a line drive and my chest is hurting." The chief complaint in this instance is chest pain. Or, "Doc, I went to the bathroom and I began to cough and there was red stuff coming from my lungs." The chief complaint is "I am coughing up blood." As a physician, you are forever thankful for direct types of communication like these because they give you firm targets that elicit a diagnostic algorithm—a step-by-step process for solving a problem.

With the baseball injury, a physician would automatically order an x-ray of the chest to look for a fracture of the sternum (breast bone). In addition, the physician would order an EKG to check for a cardiac contusion (bruise). With the second chief complaint, the steps would be to perform a chest x-ray. If that did not show anything, the physician would then order a CT scan of the chest, possibly followed by a bronchoscopy (a test that requires a flexible scope to look inside the lung passages).

These "chief complaints" elicit an almost knee jerk response that will yield a correct diagnosis to lay the foundation for proper treatment the vast majority of the time. On the other hand, the most dreaded situation I face as a physician is when I hear the words, "Doc, I don't know what it is, but I just don't feel like myself. I have no energy. I have no pep in my step. I just don't know!" When this happens, I feel some of my hair follicles pack it in and give up the ghost. This is one of the most troublesome dilemmas a physician must face in the practice of medicine. It is clear that you are facing the dreaded diagnostic enigma called malaise (mal-aise).

The source of the concern and fear that is produced by malaise is very complex. The fear comes from many factors; the most significant being the confusion generated because of not knowing the source of a cause. Malaise is a complaint shared by a variety of potential diagnoses, many of them lethal. Every illness ever coined in the history of medicine can present at some time in its course with malaise as a chief complaint.

The possibilities could range from a cold to cancer, anemia to Alzheimer's, or STD (sexually transmitted diseases) to Strep throat. Believe me, malaise is one of those things that may not necessarily kill you, but you hope you never have. When presented with this chief complaint, a doctor has to use a "shotgun approach" in ordering tests to find what the underlying cause may be. This is similar to a duck hunter, who is not a good shot, closing his eyes and shooting into the sky in the general direction of a flock hoping he will hit something.

When "shot gunning" to find a diagnosis, a doctor orders a battery of tests in hopes of finding the cause of the problem, which will guide his/her next steps. It is important to note that a shotgun is not a precise weapon, and doctors, especially surgeons, are not comfortable with this at all. Furthermore, this approach is wasteful and time consuming. But unfortunately, it is often necessary because malaise is such a nondescript, nebulous complaint. Virtually anything could be wrong, or not wrong with the patient.

Some healers fail to act on this complaint with an aggressive response. It seems like the patient's body is playing a game of hide and go seek. Of course, if you wait long enough, the diagnosis will become obvious. Unfortunately, this can be fatal for the patient.

When faced with malaise, I am gripped by fear because it could be an early sign of a life threatening illness. I instantly feel the pressure to protect my patient. I do not want to miss an opportunity to save a life.

Therefore, like most physicians, I have come up with my own system that will provide the patient with the adequate safety net they deserve.

The Rosser Doctrine of Diagnostic Dilemmas is: "If you see malaise, don't go into a daze." I have an automated reflex that goes off inside me which sounds like the robot in the old TV series *Lost in Space*, "Danger, Danger, Will Robinson please take evasive action." The proper action that can steer my patient away from death is a consistent approach to executing an exhaustive search for the cause of malaise. Then, and only then, am I able to accurately execute the proper treatment options.

Today, many feel that the United States is suffering from a chief complaint of "generalized social and economic performance malaise," which manifests itself by exhibiting subtle, but real signs of chronic underachievement and erosion of our global leadership status. And while we know that there is something wrong, we don't know exactly what it is. The symptoms include our failure to evenly distribute our wealth, in spite of America having more billionaires than at any time in history. The trickle down just seems to refuse to trickle down.

Our urban environment continues to decay and resist all our efforts to halt its devastating erosion. Both the loss and lack of jobs of substance robs citizens of the chance to claim a piece of the American dream. This haunts our country at a time when others risk their lives to illegally cross our borders to take jobs that nobody wants. Our high schools exhibit a 33 percent drop out rate and graduates flee from career choices in science, technology, engineering, math and medicine with the energy and abandon only seen in the alien attack scenes from Tom Cruise's 2005 cinema hit, *War of the Worlds*.

This concern is even more immediate in the African-American community. In Bishop James Dixon's book, *If God Is So Good, Why Are Blacks Doing So Bad?* the crisis in the African-American community is told with vivid clarity. Sixty-three percent of fourth grade black students cannot read on grade level. Sixty-one percent of African-American eighth graders cannot perform eighth-grade math. Only 56 percent of African-American students graduate high school by age 18. Only 20 percent of those who graduate high school can master college level courses. On the SAT, African-Americans score 220 points lower than Asians, 200 points less than Caucasians, and 45 points less than Hispanics.

In view of these signs and symptoms, even the most hardcore American patriot must admit that a strong case can be made that our country is not feeling or doing as well as it should. It is suffering from a generalized malaise, and we have to be concerned. Just as I am when facing a patient with malaise as a chief complaint, society must recognize that this may be an early sign of a fatal disease destined to destroy this nation. The times dictate that we must use all the assets necessary to diagnose and treat the patient as quickly as possible.

CHAPTER FIVE

THE RISE AND FALL OF A NATION: THE ANATOMY OF AMERICA'S WINNING STREAK

Many may think that I am overreacting. Some of you would say that America isn't suffering any malaise, and, even if it were, it certainly can't become fatal. This nation is not perfect and it has islands of shortcomings that have room for improvement. But does it have a serious problem?

America has long been considered the flagship of an armada of great nations that has demonstrated dominance through the course of history. Some believe that our leadership role is not in danger and I hope they are right. It is reassuring that our past points to a robust, healthy nation that can overcome any ailment, major or minor. I cannot blame anyone for having confidence in the idea of a bright future for our nation. It is true that we have a strong foundation of success. For over 200 years, the United States of America has been on one of the world's most unprecedented winning streaks. The occasional setbacks we have encountered have only been temporary blemishes to an otherwise pristine pattern of achievement.

Others have enjoyed this sort of dream team status, namely the Romans, the Ottoman Empire, the Ming Dynasty, the United Kingdom, and others. But few have done it with such a meteoric rise, with such absolute dominance, and with such a unique flair and style. At the heart of this amazing performance has been the ever-present driving force of competition and the desire to be first and the best.

Historically, Americans desire to achieve more than those who came before. We have thrived on the prospect of facing challenges with innovation and change. To examine the dynamics of America's success, one does not have to turn to historians, political scholars or theologians. The key is to look at the anatomy of a winning streak in competitive athletics, and examples of excellence in the business world.

The Birth of a Winning Streak and a Nation

In her book, *Confidence: How Winning Streaks & Losing Streaks Begin & End*, Rosabeth Moss Kanter gives intricate details about the impact of winning and winners in athletics and suggests applying these principles to successful business turnaround strategies. While her focus is on winning streaks in corporate America, I believe her suggestions also have potential applications in other aspects of society. Her book has inspired me to look at our nation's current state of societal malaise and correlate the situation to the rise and fall of a championship sports team or a successful Fortune 500 company. In Kanter's book, I believe we can find some answers to why our nation has had past success, why our successes may be coming to an end, and why we can turn this thing around.

Kanter's writings not only helped me diagnose and understand the cause of the malaise we suffer, but they also support the rationale for my treatment regimen. This includes producing a national turnaround based on my hypothesis that video games can assist in achieving corrective measures to our problems more effectively, and sooner rather than later.

When considering the cause of malaise (diagnosis of disease), you need to contrast the condition of the patient today against what the healthy patient looked like in the past. So, what did a healthy America look like? As the early settlers forged this nation from nothing, there was an inexhaustible, self-contained foundation of confidence that ran through every man, woman and child who made the journey to this new land. This established a core of individuals with like mind and undoubting purpose, laying a foundation that has served as an enduring asset for us all.

Their pioneering spirit was a great advantage in the early years of our nation because it helped to establish and maintain momentum that fueled perpetual revolutionary innovation. In business terms, the right team had been assembled and team members thrived by playing together. These early settlers were in a contest for their lives and these outcasts from other nations had no other place to go. They had to make it or die. There was no turning back. Survival can have profound effects on the tenacity of one's efforts. The early settlers of this nation forged one of Kanter's core conditions for initiating a winning streak—establishing a culture of winning. It starts with good people, a good system, and the capability of harmonic performance under pressure.

Kanter then talks about confidence and its importance in initiating and continuing winning streaks. The first type of confidence is self-confidence. The vast majority of the original colonists came to America with a past heavily laden with oppression. In their homelands, their ability to perform had been systematically hampered by a social rigidity that recognized only where they came from, not what they had the potential to do. They were born into a rigid social coffin that they were buried in at birth. Consequently, the early settlers of this nation had a pent up reservoir of suppressed energy waiting to be unleashed.

Our forefathers harbored a feeling of self-confidence that great things could happen if only they had the opportunity. They were further encouraged by the fact that under their previous circumstances, they had persevered and been productive despite minimal assistance from aristocrats and the system. Kanter points out that people who believe in themselves and thrive in the midst of competition are more likely to try harder and longer. This increases the chance of success. Individuals who succeed are more likely to believe that their efforts in the future will pay off and be rewarded.

This certainly was the case with America's first citizens. Armed with self-confidence combined with the potential and capacity to achieve, and an expectation of greatness, these pioneers planted a seed of productivity and innovation that bore fruits the likes of which had never been seen before. As Kanter says, "It is easy to find the energy to work hard because it looks as if the hard work will pay off." And for the forefathers of this nation, it did.

The importance of having confidence in ourselves cannot be underestimated as a cornerstone for America's success. During the history of the United States, its citizens have exemplified an uncanny ability, like most successful sports teams and corporations, to produce extended periods of sustained excellence. Confidence plays a very important contributing role.

Individuals and groups who are successful and win, have the ability to perform on a higher level when placed under duress. In the sports vernacular, the citizens of this country have demonstrated the ability to perform under pressure. In fact, pressure and aggressive competition bring out the best in strong sports teams, strong corporations and strong nations. Foreign powers, on more than one occasion, have made the mistake of believing that citizens of this country are a collection of mongrels without the stabilizing fabric of a common bloodline, and therefore are inherently weak and vulnerable.

The multitude of varied opinions and outspoken diversity of voices that make up our nation, present a picture of chaos and confusion to the untrained eye. But, once pressured, an amazing transformation occurs in this disparate body of people that cannot be explained by common cultural heritage. We all unite under one voice of freedom and an almost genetically ingrained desire to have self-determination. We don't want to have only one way; we want the freedom to practice many ways. We are not satiated by the opportunity of one restricted outcome. We want the ability to do better if we use our personal initiative to reach higher. We have been willing to die to assure the same opportunities for our children and their children. Like a choir, members may sing with different voices, but we all sing the same song.

Our founding fathers also had confidence in one another. This confidence helped to create positive, supportive, team-oriented behavior. For those first settlers, the journey to this country had been a very difficult one. The death rate among colonists from just the ocean passage was extremely high. Once here, they had to face the rigors of establishing shelter and a food supply before winter set in. The survivors who did not fall victim to hunger and starvation then had to face the ravages of sickness and disease. They had to depend on one another and quickly formulate a positive, supportive, team-oriented collaboration as a matter of life or death.

Every incremental success and subsequent reward was embraced, nurtured, and lauded as a flower of hope. Whether it was finding a stream for fresh water that was filled with fish to eat, or completing a dam that allowed access to very fertile land where crops could be planted, each of these circumstances represented a win that led to a reward. Wins linked in succession become a winning streak.

Kanter describes the anatomy of a winning streak in this way: "With each win, no matter how small, people feel more engaged with their task and with one another." The sense of one voice, of one purpose facilitates the perception of the occupation of common ground and a shared stake in each other's well-being; not only now, but in the future. This was important in the early days of this country. With such vast territory and isolation separating citizens, it would have been easy for this nation to self-destruct. But the rapid establishment of a national sense of "oneness" proved to be the glue that would not only keep us together, but also help us thrive.

Kanter also notes that to keep a winning streak alive, the players must have confidence in the system that they have to operate under. Democracy and a free economic system created an environment that unleashed in individuals the potential to be innovative and to effectively solve problems. This environment fueled our country's early success and continues to fuel it today. The early organizational environment of this nation featured brutal accountability, mandated collaboration, and mandatory innovation—all key components for any successful and winning endeavor.

This environment was institutionalized into our foundation as a nation with the writing of the Bill of Rights and the Constitution. The founding fathers wanted to provide a formal governmental infrastructure that would encourage institutionalized winning and success. Kanter further notes that organizational confidence helps to build a winner's habits of responsibility, teamwork and initiative; this becomes a part of all routines, processes, and practices. Everyone is able to contribute so that the team—in this case, America—can win. Furthermore, others can duplicate the success of one. Our nation has a reputation of being able to expand success to scale, and this is encouraged by democracy and the free enterprise system.

Because of these factors, there is an external confidence generated that attracts a network of outsiders who invest and provide additional resources that contribute to more wins and rewards. I call these entities "surfers" because they seek out opportunities to ride the tsunami of success that this nation has enjoyed.

The French contributed and invested during our war for independence because they wanted to get back at their arch enemy, England. They also saw the huge economic potential of being an ally with the newly formed America, rich with boundless natural resources. This tradition continues today with unprecedented outside investment from other nations that continue to pour in money to fuel the big red, white and blue machine.

From winning independence from the British, to successfully winning a war with Mexico, allowing us to expand to the Pacific ocean, to surviving a civil war that would have destroyed the average nation, to ushering in the industrial revolution, to surviving the Great Depression, to winning two world wars, withstanding two pseudo-wars, other regional conflicts, the Civil Rights Movement, and the tragedy of 9-11, the United States has been on a winning streak. This streak could be considered on par with John Wooden's UCLA basketball teams that won 10 NCAA championships—if you know anything about basketball, you know how amazing that is.

National confidence runs high because through all of our challenges as a nation, we have still managed to build the greatest economy and military force that the world has ever seen. I am not surprised that many would scoff at any chorus of warnings that the sky is falling. We are talking about the United States of America after all, the "Teflon Don" nation.

But have we finally lost our edge? Innovation, risk taking and winning got us to this point, but do we now have a sense of entitlement that has replaced our capability to work hard and be productive? Do we now possess a preoccupation with self-indulgence rather than innovation? Has competition now become the new four-letter word that is no longer politically correct to use? Has our ability to dream been replaced with the need to constantly complain and profess self-defeatism?

It is the duty of all citizens to ensure that the flagship of democracy, the United States of America, does not suffer the same fate of another colossus that was viewed to be unsinkable—the Titanic. We all know what happened when the structural integrity of that ship was breached. Winning has shaped the structural integrity of our nation, but has the framework for prosperity been breeched? We need to look at our decline as a sign of malaise, and we must rapidly make a diagnosis of the cause so treatment can begin immediately.

CHAPTER SIX

THE END OF OUR WINNINGSTREAK: OUR NATION IN DECLINE

Others may equivocate, but there is no doubt in my mind that our nation has reached the zenith of its meteoric rise to greatness and dominance as a world power.

When an airplane accelerates to full power and begins climbing to cruise altitude, the passengers are pressed back into their seats by positive G-forces that equal multiples of their body weight. When the desired altitude is reached and the airplane goes to level flight, there is a moment when you experience the sensation of weightlessness. Depending on the smoothness of the transition by the pilot, this feeling is at times not subtle. In fact, it can be very alarming to the passengers if the pilot does not show some finesse on the controls.

As a passenger, you had grown accustomed to feeling the pressure of positive G's during the ascent. If the new altitude is maintained, you will once again reach a level of comfort. If the aircraft goes on to rapidly descend, discomfort becomes alarm, which then turns into panic because all your previous reference points have been discarded. As a nation, our rocket-like ascent to sustained excellence has begun to falter, and we are experiencing the initial signs of societal weightlessness; our comfortable reference point of ascension and winning has been disturbed. Our orbit is degrading. Our nation's new challenge is to regain control and stabilize our descent until we can establish a new escape velocity and soar to even higher heights.

Timothy Garton Ash, a blog columnist insists, "Houston there is a problem, and there is a problem right now." In a January 2007 article on the Website "Comment is Free," Ash offered the argument that our malaise comes not from a leadership stalemate with the rest of the world, but rather from the fact that the United States has surrendered its leadership position and there has already been a shift of power. He not only asserts that America's winning streak is over, but strongly suggests that we are in the early stages of a possible sustained losing streak.

He sights the findings and discussions from the 2007 World Economic Forum as evidence to support his hypothesis. This meeting is meant to be a yearly snapshot of the world's problems, advancements and opportunities. The 2007 theme was "The Shifting Global Power Equation." His contention is that after the end of the Cold War, our planet became a unipolar world, with the United States as the only true superpower. In fact, a new term was invented to describe our dominance; we became a hyper-power.

At that time, the United States had no real competitors. No nation could threaten its position on top of the global food chain. Ash contends that this caused the tipping of our national confidence into unbridled arrogance, with the United States taking this coronation very seriously. Subsequently, the country adopted a more unilateral foreign policy posture. Many suggest that this is the posture taken with the Iraq War, and they question the wisdom of this position.

Ash points out that this policy is inappropriate in view of the world we live in today, because power, and the perception of power is no longer what it used to be. Today, less power resides with nations and governments. Increasingly, it exists with a number of entities that broker power through their proprietary modus operandi—multinational corporations and big banks, for example. The power map is now multi-level and multi-polar. He insists that there has been a return to where the world was before the United States ruled supreme.

I agree with Ash's argument. He is using the Internet, a non-traditional source of news and information, to get his message heard. In my opinion, this illustrates exactly what he is talking about. The unthinkable has happened in the news industry. There has been a shift of the power signature and the way individuals access information. The Internet enables those who were previously muted by the system to have a voice that the masses can hear. My response to this is that there is no cause to freak out because we now have to share our power.

During most of history, power has been shared. It has been only recently that the West has wielded a dominant focus. But now, we are in the age of global realignment assisted in large part, by the advent of the digital age.

Today, Asia is on the upward move. Its ascent is signaled by the emergence of China and India as global players. A January 2007 Time Magazine article has already announced the "Dawn of a New Dynasty" with the seat of power being located in Beijing. The United States has become a casualty of the economic game that it created. This is translating into a shifting of the economic and military power base to the East. This presents a challenge of substantial proportions because these bustling accelerating economies are now competing with the United States for energy, raw materials and manpower. Barring technological breakthroughs and societal adjustments, there is only going to be so much to go around. The Asian renaissance and energy race will shape the new global power structure.

Also to be considered is the emergence of non-state players such as terrorist organizations that are empowered by new technologies and oil currency. They are also demanding a piece of the pie. The scenarios presented in the hit show *24* are far-out possibilities of the influence of these new power brokers, but this fruit of friction does not fall far from the tree of truth. I agree with Ash's assertions that the United States is not the dominant power broker in the new and ever changing world of today, and that this condition must not be allowed to stand.

There is more evidence of the erosion of our influence. Kanter suggests that one of the luxuries of a successful winning sports program is the ability to have the best of the best wanting to come and join your team. The process of recruiting is made much easier in the face of a perennial winning ball club. A team's ability to recruit or attract good talent helps it to maintain a winning edge. The loss of this ability is a telltale sign of imminent decline. The influx of great athletes wanting to join your team is a barometer of how well your program is doing.

Winning programs always seem to have a never-ending supply of new talent that helps to maintain a team's winning tradition. In the past, students would come to the United States to become educated and fight 'tooth and nail' to stay. They did not want to go back home. Now the reverse is true. Foreign students come here, get educated, and then go back to their homelands. Today, there has been a flow reversal of human resources and innovative energy. We don't have our pick of the best of the best anymore.

To compound the problem of this auxiliary brain drain (the exodus of talented foreign human resources), we also are in the midst of a primary brain drain. One of the most glaring areas of deficiency is represented by the nation not cultivating its own to step up in the important career choices of science, technology, engineering, and mathematics (STEM).

With the United States not attracting the best and brightest from outside our borders, we cannot afford the luxury of ignoring our own vast untapped reservoir of assets. Our challenge will be attracting these groups and others to serve as an influx of new talent with different perspectives. Now I will gladly listen to any argument that will convince me that the societal malaise and circumstances that currently grip our nation are figments of my imagination. I would love for someone to credibly reassure me that our winning streak as a world power is not over. But frankly, I do not think the case can be easily made.

With all due respect to those of you still struggling with the notion that we aren't winning anymore, the challenge to America's record of perennial winning should come as no surprise to any of us. Kanter warns that it is hard to win forever because there are many natural and man-made factors that, by design, breed and assist competition. The Asian renaissance represents the classic paradox of success. We encouraged and taught them how to play the economic game. Our success created attractive markets, which encouraged imitation, and brought out the passion of others to do the same as us, and better. Their actions are fueled by the desire to compete and win because of the profound expanse of the potential rewards. They not only want to "be like Mike," they want to "be better than Mike."

This cultural medium helps to create innovation frenzy. All entities that dominate a space must have and maintain a baseline level of innovation that contributes greatly to their keeping an edge over the competition. Initially, innovators and pioneers have the field to themselves, but one should count on and expect others to rapidly jump in. In order to be "better than Mike," they are driven to invest the time, energy and money to make that dream become a reality. You may ask the questions, "Why do they want to be like us?" "Doesn't the rest of the world hate us?" On the surface this may seem to be the case, but the answer is much more complex. The rest of the world may not be happy with our political policies, but they love our pop culture. They think our stuff is cool. And you must never underestimate the power of cool!

For a long time, I did not understand this disconnect. You hate us, but you love our stuff?! Initially, I struggled with this notion, but it should not have come as a surprise. There is no place on Earth where America and our pop culture have not reached. We have branded ourselves as the cradle of cool! Could there be more potential for peace using MTV rather than firing a depleted Uranium shell from a tank? The power of the prospect of marketing and MTV being a nuclear deterrent is not as far-fetched as it sounds!

I will never forget being in Africa, driving down a dirt road and passing some villagers. Two boys stood out in the crowd. Both looked to be around age 12. I singled them out because one had on a Michael Jordan t-shirt, and the other had a t-shirt that read, "I love my MTV." I waved and smiled, and I pointed to the image of his "Airness" on the first boy's chest. He instinctively stopped walking and began to dribble with an invisible basketball. He then jumped up into the air mimicking Jordan's patented fade away jump shot, tongue wagging and all. I doubt that this kid had ever touched a real basketball. I then pointed to the other boy's chest and he instantly fashioned his hands as if he was holding a microphone. He then began to move his lips as if he was spitting out rhymes and performing in a Tupac Shakur rap video. He may not have seen a television in his life, but he knew about MTV.

Our global marketing campaigns are so effective that even people in the most remote areas become exposed to our culture. Not only do they develop a strong attraction to it, but they also start interpreting our culture in a way that fits their societal and cultural parameters. Our effective marketing campaigns serve a purpose similar to that of the mechanical rabbit at a dog race, and the rest of the world is always chasing the rabbit. Eventually, if a leader holds their pace, the student catches and begins to school the teacher. Why can't we leverage this cycle of winning and losing, to once again earn the right to lead in the global community?

An example of how our success can be our worst enemy can be seen by looking at how the rest of the world is catching up with the United States in basketball. Our competitive edge in the game that we invented is slowly but surely slipping away. All of this began with a conscious effort by the NBA to globalize the game of basketball. They wanted to expand in order to harvest more profit. But an interesting thing happened on the way to the bank. The rest of world not only gained interest, but they also began to morph the game to represent their own cultural interpretation of what the game should be.

The rest of the world believed that the game should be one of finesse and a demonstration of skill. The international community did not feel that the constant display of force and power should negate the execution of great play. Therefore, international rules widened the lane to make the court less congested. International teams concentrate on the art of passing and shooting the basketball. Three point shot attempts are emphasized and encouraged. In the last few Olympics and international competitions, the United States was put in a position of having to play catch up.

The Downfall of a Dynasty, Winning Comes to an End

Often, the very nature of success produces competition that will eventually challenge continued dominance. This is how it should be and it is not necessarily the death certificate of a nation. I could rant on and on about the global decline of American dominance, but a more constructive option would be to investigate how Rosabeth Kanter looks at why a winning streak comes to an end in athletics and the business world. This is necessary so that a correlation can be made when we consider interventions that can lead to a harvest of winning once again.

Usually a team, a business, or even a country has an opportunity see the end coming long before losing starts. But, the fog of denial conceals the first steps toward oblivion. When faced with the initial suggestions of a less than ideal state of affairs, a standard knee jerk reaction is prompted and a man-hunt begins to locate any and all excuses to discredit the obvious signs of a retreat from established performance standards. This serves to mask the presence of serious issues, and delays the recognition of the need for immediate attention to these items.

When this happens, everyone strives to maintain the status quo or "I want to feel good right now mode." No one likes for it to rain on his or her parade. To put this into terms of the nation, the idea that we have a right to the same great horn of plenty as our forefathers can be dangerous. Because we have been winning for so long, we can take winning for granted. Kanter points out that when people get complacent about winning, they stop executing all the little things that are responsible for their success in the first place. In other words, when you become comfortable with mediocrity, there is a persona of timidity that takes over. You are no longer the aggressive, innovative, "no problem is too big to beat" water walker. You become a person who is comfortable sitting in a rocking chair on the front porch, expecting the rewards of life to be brought to you, and brothers and sisters, nothing will get done from there.

In our country today, we have been winning for so long, we're sitting in our collective rocking chairs. Too many of us think that winning is our birthright, an entitlement, and we seem determined to drink champagne even through there is only one bottle left.

Kanter goes on to point out that once a team is inoculated with the virus of denial, there is a subsequent decrease in dialogue—nobody wants to talk about the problem. Nobody wants to admit that anything is wrong, so everybody stops communicating with one another. Therefore, the problem never gets identified, let alone addressed, and ways to fix the problem are not explored. Granted, open admission of a less than stellar review of a state of affairs is not what many would rank up there as the most pleasurable thing to look forward to upon waking in the morning.

Bad news is like an ugly suitor who is very fond of you, but frankly you would rather not go out with so you just tend to shy away. But a nation can never shy away from communication and open dialogue, because this supports the continuation of accountability, collaboration and initiative. These are absolute prerequisites for winning, continuing to win, and the re-establishment of a winner.

As Kanter suggests, without dialogue, denial becomes a state of being that only hastens your spiral downward. If the team will not discuss their challenges as a group, teammates retreat into their own sub-groups, so they can communicate their own version of the truth about their situation. In these groups, there is an orgy of finger pointing. Then respect for everyone outside the sub-group decreases, further widening rifts. This fuels a move toward isolationism. Each sub-group then circles the wagons to protect their turf. Turfism makes the partitioning of the team, company, or country complete with the end of success and winning not being far behind. These are the grisly details of the depth of a nation before it takes its final breath.

Another reason why winning streaks and periods of dominance come to an end is that winning can become boring. High expectations mean that a winning team gets to a point where they receive muted credit for victory. This inadvertently removes some of the initiative that is promoted by reward. It becomes very difficult to see the reward and the prospects of reward, real or perceived. Make no mistake; reward is one of the main driving forces behind the achievement of dominance. To add to this, it seems that the more one wins, the more others become "haters," and being hated is definitely not cool.

Just look at the legacy of dominance by the New York Yankees in baseball; they have won 26 world championships. No one matches the Yankees' level of sustained excellence in competitive athletics. But they get no love from those outside New York. They are the team that everyone loves to hate. No matter whom they put out on the field, the Yankees project a symbol of superiority, and it elicits a love/hate reaction that mutes the upside of reward.

I believe to some extent that there is an element of what is discussed above happening in the United States today. Despite our winning personas, the upside of reward is muted. We're used to winning, and in some ways, winning has become boring to us. We expect this symbol of excellence without an appreciation of the hard work that goes hand in hand with winning.

Regardless of this state of affairs, as a nation we must stay the course. We must once again practice the hard work and perseverance that started the winning in the first place. All winning streaks are threatened when confidence changes to arrogance, and the blaze of complacency is fueled by the crippling enigma of entitlement.

Kanter's portrait of a fall from the ranks of success is absolutely on target. In medicine—to go back to that metaphor—many diseases happen insidiously without warning. There are only subtle signs and symptoms that frequently go unnoticed. At this point, the patient is experiencing a chief complaint of general malaise. The victim, in spite of not feeling well, continues to loiter in a state of denial until they collapse and the diagnosis becomes crystal clear. Tragically, the person had been experiencing the warning signs of a deadly disease and did not know it. Unfortunately, when this happens, it is often too late for treatment.

At this crucial time in our history, we must recognize the warning signs and symptoms of performance malaise, make a correct diagnosis, and execute a treatment strategy that will cure the patient (nation) of the disease. The cessation of a winning streak is not the result of a single factor; multiple factors converge at a strategic moment in time to bring success to a screeching halt. And multiple resources must be used in order to turn our fortunes around, even non-traditional assets that have never been used before.

Mistakes of policy and purpose by themselves do not make winners become losers. In the final analysis, from Kanter's vantage point, the factors you face are not of ultimate importance, but it is your response to the inevitability of adversity that makes the difference. In essence, winning streaks come to an end because of what a team (business or nation) does to itself and not necessarily the challenges they face. Mistakes, losses and setbacks should only be temporary impediments to a person, team, company or country that remains committed to the system that brought them their success in the first place.

It is key for any winning team to be able to play under pressure. They must continue to maintain an inspired effort in the face of challenge. During this time of great national uncertainty, keep in mind that winning is a constant struggle, and for the United States, it is vital that we continually remember to forge on, and *play to win*. Because if we don't, it is not an issue of *if* our winning streak and success will come to an end, but a matter of *when*.

Optimally, this threat should be met with a sense of familiarity and ever-present calm accompanied by a drive to excel. Panic is the lynchpin of defeatism fueled by the fact that panic and good decision-making cannot constructively co-exist. Panic must be suppressed at all costs because it is contagious. The panic of a few can cause the chaos of many, and chaos is the master key that opens the door to failure. How one performs under pressure defines greatness and ultimately establishes dynasties.

When all is said and done, it is the implementation of adjustments to a challenge that will make the ultimate difference. These adjustments frequently involve maturing and embracing resources that previously had been thought to have no value at all. The cure for our societal malaise will be defined by our ability to identify creative solutions to deeply entrenched problems.

The good news is that we have done it before and we have the ability to do it again. But we must quicken our pace in this race, for it is always a race to stay on top; there are only temporary winners. We must elevate the intensity of effort and search for the edge of innovation. Above all, we must know that we are at "mission critical" status and we must be willing to use any asset or tactic without prejudice that will help turn our fortunes around; even if that asset is a vilified pop-culture icon like video games.

It is my profound belief that the incorporation of various aspects and features of video game techniques, tactics and culture into mainstream society could assist in the treatment and reversal of our national performance malaise. I can hear skeptics gasp in disbelief, but the start of the journey down the road to the renewed good health of our nation could start that simply. In the words of a great American, Al Davis, the owner of the Oakland Raiders, "All you have to do is maintain a commitment to excellence and just win baby."

Part Three

THE FUTURE OF OUR NATION: WHAT DO VIDEO GAMES HAVE TO DO WITH IT?

● ● ● ●

So, how do we start winning again? And, what do video games really have to do with it? How can something that millions of people indulge in everyday reinvigorate the spirit of America's first settlers—the overwhelming drive to succeed? The answer lies in the very nature of what video games do to the person playing them. It lies in both the content of the game, and the physical reactions that happen when a person actually gets their hands on the joystick and starts playing.

In Rosabeth Kanter's book, *Confidence*, she details the intricacies of how success and winning are nurtured, whether associated with a sports team, or corporation. In the previous chapter, I took lessons forged from her respected vantage point, and applied these principles to the state of our nation today and the path to excellence in the future. In this section I suggest that video games can facilitate and deliver important validated turnaround components that do not just apply to the salvation of sports teams or corporations, but also can be the messiah for a nation as well.

In her book, Kanter lists and discusses categories of stepping-stones that must be engaged in order to be successful in any "come from behind" situation. These include: the grooming of the proper culture, the cultivation of collaboration, and addressing the challenge of disseminating inspiration and innovation. I present my argument that video games could play a significant role in fulfilling many of these criteria.

CHAPTER SEVEN
THE DRIVE TO WIN: IT'S IN OUR BLOOD

When blessed with an asset, one should feel mandated to use that advantage to the hilt. Video game play taps into a natural biochemical mechanism that oversees a behavioral framework that makes us competitive, innovative, and willing to put out maximum effort to seek reward.

Steven Johnson is a pop culture advocate who has looked deeply into the upside of pop culture. In his book, *Everything Bad Is Good For You*, he elaborates on a powerful physiological fact to explain some of the extraordinary effects that video games have on human beings, especially our inherent compulsion to compete and win. He discusses how video games activate a chemical feedback loop in the brain that actually enhances the attractiveness and thrill to the process of winning. In short, he argues that video games tap into the brain's natural reward circuitry.

The lynchpin of this phenomenon is something called dopamine. In the brain, dopamine keeps track of levels of reward parameters. When the rewards don't come in, it sends out a notice or alert in the form of lowered dopamine levels. This response announces that your reward account is low. Next, the lowered dopamine levels caused by a shortfall of rewards, trigger cravings, and these cravings drive you to do whatever it takes to elevate the dopamine to the desired level.

The nerve center for this pattern is called the dopamine-adrenergic system and it is located in the nucleus accumbens, a microscopic anatomical portion of the brain. This structure stands at the helm of the brain's reward seeking circuitry. This circuitry is a survival character trait left over from our evolution from hunter-gathers. The craving for that which you do not have but want and/or need, drives you to seek out the acquisition of these items with extreme prejudice. And if you don't find it, the brain just tells you to look harder.

Dopamine is the key conduit for fulfilling the brain's duty to provide checks, balances and oversight, which are pivotal to sustaining life. It is also intimately connected to our internal reward system. Johnson suggested that dopamine is like an accountant, but I think of dopamine as an Internal Revenue Service auditor. Both entities can evaluate, and alert one to the presence of inconsistencies. But, the Internal Revenue Service can also initiate and execute corrective action. This is the case with dopamine.

As a surgeon, I must deal with this system on an ongoing basis in order to assist in a patient's healing process. I frequently find myself as a conductor of a healing symphony, dynamically manipulating different sections of the dopamine-adrenergic orchestra to maintain the life of a patient. If the pulse of a patient is too low, I will use a drug that promotes the pulse to elevate to desired levels. This measure can also be used if the blood pressure is too low and you want to return it to a normal level. At times, I will become totally immersed in this elaborate symphony that is being conducted on the microvascular level as I work to utilize the dopamine-adrenergic system to attain a healing steady-state that will stabilize a patient and give them a chance to become well again.

Video games, with their constant effort and reward cycle, stimulate the dopamine-adrenergic system. In other words, they tap into a system that already exists in our body's chemistry. Now, some use the aggressive drive for and the quest to attain a continuous presence of reward, to explain the seemingly hypnotic and possible addictive nature of video games. This has even prompted some in the medical profession and the American Medical Association (AMA) to declare that a separate diagnostic designation should be created for those who suffer from video game addiction.

The doctors who are seeking to declare this as a new diagnosis are doing so against the backdrop of tragic school shootings—Columbine and Virginia Tech—as society searches relentlessly for an explanation for the unthinkable. Some assert that these shootings happened because of a video game culture gone out of control. The fact that the AMA is looking to designate this new diagnosis is very disturbing to me, because physicians know that there is evidence to suggest that these school shooting cases are not the result of a primary video game addiction, but rather the video game component is secondary to a primary mental disorder or personality disturbance. There are already established diagnostic parameters for these disease states.

I believe that creating a special disease category will fuel hysteria and hang another noose around the neck of video game culture. Unfortunately, this type of behavior is typical for the establishment when it concerns video games, and it serves to fan the fires of a video game witch hunt that is predicated on fear. A huge disservice is committed because it retards understanding the real power of video games and adds another barrier of inertia to the utilization of their positive collateral learning assets.

I am not a social revolutionary, but I want to charge full speed ahead and saturate society with any positive influence that video games have to offer. As a scientist, I know that the successful capture of the positive aspects of the dopamine system with video games will require the performance of proper scientific due diligence. True to my medical heritage, my goal is to try to identify and harness features that could have a healing impact for my patients. My response as a parent is the very personal commitment to doing all I can to make sure that my children, grandchildren, and yours, have a stable platform to conduct their drive to capture the American dream.

As you can imagine, I have at times been accused of being very candid, as well as an eternal optimist. I am always bluntly describing the cup and always insisting that it is half full rather than half empty. My optimism is justified. I have seen what video games can do for surgery. Video game-assisted training can teach a surgeon faster and more effectively than ever before. This not only potentially saves millions of dollars but untold numbers of lives as well. Being able to tie off a bleeding vessel in two minutes saves lives; Period! All things can be harnessed for the greater good if we look hard enough—even a primordial neural response mechanism like the dopamine-adrenergic system.

CHAPTER EIGHT

GROOMING A NEW CULTURE:
GOING BACK TO THE FUTURE

In order to reinvigorate our spirit of competition with the dogged determinism of our forbearers—and turn our losing streak back into a winning one, we need something that will bring us back into a culture of institutionalized winning. I believe that the spark can be found in video games.

As a nation, we've gone soft. We have been slowly but surely retreating from a focus on competition and winning for many decades. All those who have come before us created this luxury: the settlers, the pioneers and innovators. These are the heroes that made this nation great. They forged for us a cushion that is made up of their hard work, dogged determination, creativity, and exemplary leadership, mixed with a sacrificial element of blood, sweat and tears.

Sadly, we under appreciate the fact that today's America stands on the shoulders of these giants who paid a stiff price, starting with the signers of the Declaration of Independence who were ostracized for their belief in a nation free to choose how to govern itself. The sacrifice continued with the men and women who forged this nation out of a wilderness, and is memorialized by those who made the ultimate sacrifice. The generations that have come before us shaped a powerful and stable union. Is today's generation ready to mount the same response when confronted with some of the staunch challenges that our nation faces today? Many feel we have become complacent and have forgotten that we must have the same commitment to forge ahead like our forefathers.

I believe that video games are an unexplored wilderness that possesses a wealth of natural resources that can help our nation.

These seemingly mindless forms of entertainment actually have the ability to incorporate advantageous resources into our society, and implement countermeasures that can restore our winning cycle. These include a renewed focus on competition, winning and reward, the re-emergence of an insatiable appetite for the exploration of the unknown, a return to a strenuous work ethic partnered with a willingness to accept delayed gratification, and being able to turn losing into winning.

Our current education and training systems will be the major beneficiaries. This is where the battle will be fought for the future of our nation. I am not suggesting these strategic areas should be totally dismantled. But they are in need of a major upgrade, if we are to meet the demands of a nation struggling to rediscover its *mojo*.

To try to explain my position, I would like to go back to what I do for a living: treating patients. If a patient has been diagnosed with a serious infection, it is a medically known fact that antibiotics need to be given. The critical decision doctors immediately face is which route of delivery should be used. Will it be given by mouth or through the veins (intravenously)? If the infection were serious, it would be inappropriate to give the antibiotics by mouth. The absorption from the stomach is too slow and incomplete and the levels in the blood are not strong enough to fight off a serious infection. When treating a patient with a serious infection, the medicine should be administered through a route that will take it to all parts of the body very quickly in very effective levels.

Education and training impact all aspects of society. It is the core of our nation's industrial economic productivity and military readiness. If video games are going to help change our current culture and execute Kanter's requirements for a turnaround, we must use them to impact the way we educate and train our citizens.

When we think of education in this country, we think of a process that transfers facts to students that they retain as proven by traditional testing. Video games can do more than educate—now sit up and pay attention—

they can empower us. And the two are not the same. Being in possession of information by itself is not the high ground that we seek. The Holy Grail is being able to possess information and dynamically apply it to real world circumstances. That is empowerment. Video games can help us take whatever we have learned in an educational setting and help us apply it with competence and confidence in the real world. They can allow us to go into virtual environments and put the facts we learned to the test in real world situations.

The only difference is that in the virtual world, experience can be gained without suffering the consequences of making a mistake. Imagine learning without the fear of failure? You can practice before you have to do it for real. The influence of simulator-based (experiential) learning has been one of the reasons for the aerospace industry performing with unprecedented efficiency and accuracy.

A society with an education and training system that is heavily influenced by the positive assets of video game could erode boredom and detachment from the learning process. If more individuals were captured by the motivation of competition, winning, reward and the intrigue of real-world relevance, more of them would be attracted and not repulsed by the system. We will then see a wide range of individuals recruited into critical career choices that will power our drive back to the top.

To conclude my point, an increasing amount of evidence is being uncovered that identifies a video game's ability to more effectively establish individual skill and knowledge. My long-standing belief that video games are a powerful teacher that can help steer a revolution of change is now starting to be backed up by science.

More Video Game Dots That Connect to the Greater Good

If we could incorporate the features of video games into our nation's landscape, we could not only reinvigorate our spirit of competition, we could re-establish a culture of excitement over the prospects of exploring the expanse of the unknown. Steven Johnson talks about this with great enthusiasm. In *Everything Bad is Good for You*, he highlights the features of video games that could impact the greater good. A society that embraces video game culture could rekindle the thrill of the hunt and open up new frontiers to explore.

Video games leverage the tease of unraveling the mystery of new things and drive one to continually put forth effort. When you are hooked on playing a video game, it is because of the most elemental form of desire, the desire to see the next thing. We are natural explorers. Video game play takes advantage of, and cultivates this tendency, like a farmer planting new crops in the spring and being excited with the anticipation of a bountiful harvest in the fall. America in the past has thrived on seeking and finding the next best thing first. Regardless of the subject matter, Americans love to be immersed in the process of exploration, success and reward. Video games offer the unique cocktail of exploration of the unknown for the hope of reward.

Another feature of video game play that can be recycled into society is the concept of hard work as the cornerstone of success. I know, some of you are thinking, "What???" But please bear with me. There is a misconception that video games are all fun and games. This is an opinion usually held by persons who have never played these types of games or have just been casual observers. A person who has never fully engaged in a video game cannot adequately understand the effort that is being exerted by a player.

There is a raging inferno of activity that lies beneath the seemingly mindless stare and random moving of a mouse or joystick. These games are hard work, and the effort can go on for hours. Anything that can motivate a person to willingly invest such a large amount of time and effort has to be captured for the advancement of the greater good of society.

In addition to promoting hard work, video games help the player endure hardship and failure in order to receive a reward down the road for their efforts. Any serious video game player has to develop a profound ability to practice delayed gratification. In many, many games, from *Donkey Kong* to *World of Warcraft*, you have to be prepared to taste defeat many times over before you can truly enjoy the game. Video games can take an individual who would normally pull out their hair if they have to wait on a person in a wheelchair to cross the street, and have them patiently going through the drudgery of clearing out an endless number of boars ("World of Warcraft") to advance to next play level.

Name another circumstance where you see such a profound transformation. For me, the thought of delayed gratification being advanced by video games is simply amazing, absolutely amazing! It is not a far reach for one to believe that a curriculum featuring this aspect of video game play could produce a learning environment where the student is patient, focused, and stays on task. Now from where I stand, a solid work ethic and a willingness to endure delayed gratification are traits that this nation has shown in the past and what we should be about today, and in the future. Regardless of the source, we need to study the magic of video games, bottle it and distribute it to everybody.

In video game culture, losing is a necessary part of a process that leads to winning and being successful. Competition presents us with the opportunity to win. But more importantly, it puts us in a position to lose. Video gamers use losing as an ally that shapes their ability to be successful when presented with the next challenge. Losing gives us an opportunity to learn and adapt. The knowledge gained becomes the fabric of what makes up the most highly coveted deliverable that we extract from the process of competition. Losing, not winning, is the bedrock of success.

The opportunity to have meaningful, significant, and long-lasting success is better served from enduring encounters of painful, hard-fought losses, than from an obligatory parade of easy wins. Rosabeth Kanter points out that this ability to learn from losing and to make proper adjustments is the key to turning around any losing streak or corporation.

One of the greatest mistakes we can make is to think that the promotion of competition as a driving force for a renewal in the upward momentum of this nation, is all about winning property, wealth or fame. Winning comes in many forms and is not a pie with homogenous consistency. Winning must be looked at as a layer cake, where one layer is nothing without the other if you are to be successful in creating a memorable delicacy. In order to win, a blend of coordinated efforts must assist each other in obtaining a designated goal.

There is a very popular commercial featuring Michael Jordan, probably the greatest basketball player of all time. Of course, there have been many commercials that have chronicled his great career. But there was one that serves to illustrate the impact of losing on the evolution of winning and greatness. Jordan, of course, is the personification of the quintessential winner. Not because of his championship rings, but because of the package of character traits that illustrate what losing can spawn.

This commercial did not spotlight his extraordinary athletic talent. It did not feature his graceful physique. It did not concentrate on his legacy of winning. This commercial was special because it chose instead to spotlight his failures. It dramatically recanted the body of his situations and shortcomings. Failures forged his legend because they served to inspire in him the development of determination, perseverance, self-evaluation and honesty, as well as creative techniques, mature tactics, and a willingness to explore new frontiers to become great and stay great. The lessons learned from failure are mainstays of the nature of video game play and if this nation is to thrive, we must learn how to take this asset into all levels of society.

If you look at our nation from the outside in, it appears that we are more concerned about protecting our interests from the turmoil of failure rather than embracing the risks that must be taken with winning. This can be seen in all aspects of our country, from the education of our children, to our economic and foreign policy. We must reverse this trend, draw closer to our nation's competitive roots, and suppress our fear of failure. We must re-kindle our love affair with risk-taking. As in video game play, losing must become looked upon as a transient state that one must encounter along a journey that leads to the achievement of one's goals.

Video gamers live with the prospect of losing on a moment-to-moment basis. It is not only accepted, but it is not feared. Each player knows that it is necessary and temporary because it can reveal the key to ultimate victory.

Video gamers aren't the only ones who understand this principle. Military strategists use this technique as a standard practice. Frequently, they will probe an enemy's defenses and risk limited losses in order to gauge their enemy's strength and tactics. They then use that information to formulate a battle plan that has a higher potential of being successful. Even Thomas Edison knew of the power of losing. He took more than 10 years and 20,000 experiments to invent a light, durable, efficient battery.

At one point, someone questioned his reasoning: "Mr. Edison, you have failed 20,000 times. What makes you think you will get results?" Mr. Edison's reply was, "Results? Why, I've got a lot of results. I know 20,000 things that don't work." Video games can reload the spirit of Thomas Edison. Let's embrace what they have to offer so that our nation can once again return to a culture of winning.

CHAPTER NINE

CULTIVATING COLLABORATION: THE NEW ERA OF COLLABORATIVE COMPETITION

One criticism of what I have presented so far might be that the mantra "win at all costs" is totally not cool today. In fact, a person who is intensely competitive is almost looked upon as having a clandestine psychiatric disorder. From every player in little league getting a trophy, win or lose, to our institutions of higher learning shifting to pass/fail grading systems, there is a definite push back from competition and a push towards making everyone equal.

This system blurs the lines between winners and losers. (By the way, doesn't this smell a little like communism? And didn't that system fail?) To be fair, I cannot simply dismiss the other side of the competition coin—the hysterical over-reactions that can occur in the overly competitive. Indeed, if a society becomes fixated, there are negative aspects to a fanatical cycle of competition and reward. We all can see the replays on You Tube of the irate parent who snaps, goes into a state of temporary insanity and rushes out to clobber a football player who just made a great tackle on his child.

In addition, good citizenship becomes a casualty of a society totally consumed by the, "I won't participate unless you can show me what's in it for me mentality." But, this doesn't have to be an "either/or" proposition. To reinvigorate us, we need a type of competition that is constructive, not destructive like the aforementioned irate parent. I propose that we consider a new twist to the definition of competition. It is a kinder, gentler version that is becoming more and more respected as the facilitator of a paradigm shift in the way we approach massive, complex challenges. It is the concept of *collaborative competition*, and, you guessed it, it is the kind of competition that has its origin in video games.

I would like to go over some definitions. *Collaboration* is a process defined by the interaction of knowledge and mutual learning between two or more people who are working together in an intellectual endeavor toward a common goal, which is typically creative in nature. *Competition* is the act of challenge for the purpose of demonstrating superior skill or knowledge. Competitions may be between two or more forces, systems, individuals, or groups. Collaborative competition is different because it uses competition to focus team effort on a designated problem. Collaborative competition has been hailed as the most powerful form of competition a free economy has ever known. It is noteworthy because of its potential to be a vehicle that can lead to solving some of society's most perplexing problems in previously unthinkable accelerated timetables. Solving a very complex investigative challenge is the objective rather than the glory of an individual's discovery of findings.

In collaborative competitions, there is strong motivation for participants to help one another reach goals by providing feedback, answering questions, and working as a distributed group. Collaborative competition encourages participants to become skilled at managing projects, developing teambuilding skills, improving problem-solving, as well as interpersonal skills. This type of competition provides a constructive approach in the quest to capture the positive aspects of competition, winning, and the race to be first, while encouraging good sportsmanship, perseverance and strategic thinking. Think of a nation or world where these attributes are exhibited throughout society.

The upside of collaborative competition is expansive. The willingness to share and receive information gives "collaborative competition" participants the ability to rapidly develop primary responses and reason through multiple courses of action to secure their goals. This strategic ability increases the probability of success by increasing the ability to make better decisions.

Improved decision-making is an attribute that spills over into a participant's everyday life and is invaluable when faced with life's changes, obstacles, and disappointments. The participant is better able to handle the constant barrage from day-to-day background noise and subsequently becomes more efficient in interpreting data. In addition, this predilection for clarity leads to an ability to see, plan, rehearse, revise and incorporate new ideas easily instead of rejecting or discarding them.

Collaborative competition allows us to corral inherent competitive tendencies and direct that energy into a more constructive enterprise. The negative aspects of competition are suppressed while the positive aspects are amplified. The team is first and the individuals that make up the team are focused on being first to contribute something of significance to help the team shine. There is competition—fierce competition— but it is all part of a colossal unified effort.

The problem faced by the team is so immense that every effort is tempered by the knowledge that no one person or group will be responsible for the final answer. There is no one great breakthrough, no one towering genius to take all the glory. Because the end requires a team effort, competition is compartmentalized and directed not at other individuals or even other teams, but at solving the problem at hand. This does not mean that there is no room for individual recognition. As the investigative journey progresses towards a solution, there are plenty of smaller challenges that need to be addressed before the project is over. Ultimately, everyone will have a fair opportunity to claim their share of success and victories.

I do believe that if we are to take back our position as the "best of the best," we need to reinstate a culture of competition, but the kind of competition that leads to more problems being solved and not more problems being added. I want everyone to relax when they consider my call for a renewed proximity to the drive to win because there is nothing wrong with a little "collaborative competition" between friends.

Collaborative Competition and On-Line Video Gaming

Online video games are hugely popular and are excellent examples of "collaborative competitions" where teamwork, good sportsmanship, and strategic thinking are a must if you are going to win. Online video game environments allow players to meet, communicate, interact and process large amounts of information. All of this is done while simultaneously manipulating virtual worlds where participants seek social interaction and competition. Do I think that collaborative competition promoted through video games can have a positive impact on our nation's turnaround? You bet I do! Read on.

Online games began in the 1980s with simple multiplayer text-based games, often played on a bulletin board service using a modem. They have now evolved from the exclusive domain of computer geeks into something rewarding for everyone. Because of the advancement in computing power and the Internet, individuals of all ages and from all walks of life are now spending thousands of hours and dollars partaking in this popular new brand of escapism. Most industry analysts agree that online games will continue to grow in raw usage, and will generate significant revenue.

Revenue has grown to $5.2 billion with continued steady growth. By 2009, online gaming revenue worldwide will reach $9.8 billion. With millions of people actively playing online games, companies are investing millions of dollars into online game development. Marc Prensky, CEO of Games2Train and author of *Digital Game-Based Learning*, contends that individuals are growing up with online games as a primary form of interactive entertainment and there is opportunity to use this as an empowerment asset.

Such Massive OnLine MultiPlayer (MOLMP) games as "World of Warcraft" and "Second Life," attract millions of players from around the world at any given moment of the day. They are all caught up in collaborating and competing in interactive and visually rich environments, while at the same time using an array of data manipulation and online communication tools.

"World of Warcraft" is a form of collaborative competition that allows players to develop and demonstrate the ability to think strategically, cooperate as a group/team, and improve social skills. "World of Warcraft" chronicles a struggle between the Alliance (humans, dwarfs, gnomes and elves) and the Horde (orcs, tauren, trolls and undead). The game allows the player to acquire any two trade skills that can be used in different ways to contribute to the war effort. This includes such tasks as being a healer or a tradesman that can skin and create leatherwork. These items can be used acutely to support a battle or stockpile for use later. Often there will be an inventory of items that are very desirable to others because no battle can be won without these items. It should come as no surprise that there is a World of Warcraft Economy (WOWECON) that is this virtual world's New York Stock Exchange. Prices and volume of transactions can be followed at the touch of a button.

This game's popularity is immense. To date, over 10 million players participate worldwide, (2.5 million players in North America, two million players in Europe, and 3.5 million players in China alone) and this number is growing every month. Why not use a modified format and storyline in the game to promote Kanter's components for a turnaround?

That's right, not all of these collaborative competition online games have to do with war. "Second Life" is another online game that involves a "collaborative" environment, which received international attention in late 2006 and early 2007. It is an exciting online "social simulation" game that features a collaborative format that shows great potential for education and training. Since its debut, it has grown explosively, and today is inhabited by more than seven million people. Individuals can interact with each other as avatars, with a network of social interactions allowing "residents" to socialize, participate in activities, create, and trade services and items such as virtual property.

Players can play darts, chess or any other game that they desire. They can also create their own games. Players with superior technical skills can create items such as cars and sell them to people who are in need of transportation in the game. The "Second Life" marketplace currently supports millions of U.S. dollars in monthly transactions by allowing virtual currency (the Linden Dollar) to be used and exchanged for goods and services. All types of items in the real world are available for exchange. This is now coming under scrutiny from the Internal Revenue Service. Could it be that there will be a place on a future tax return for income and transactions in the virtual world?

My point is that online video gaming and virtual worlds have become established real world players, all because of the power of global competitive collaboration. The infrastructure has been established and tested and is ready to spread and penetrate into mainstream society. This network that was originally established for mere entertainment is primed to help advance public welfare.

Inspiration of Initiative and Innovation

Collaborative competition using the power of the Internet to change the world is certainly heady stuff. But do not place an undue amount of attention on the technical backdrop of collaborative competition. This would overlook the most significant element it has to offer, one of Kanter's stepping-stones to a successful sports team or corporation turnaround: the inspiration of initiative that spawns innovation.

The best example I can think of to illustrate the potential of collaborative competition is the Human Genome Project (HGP). This project also illuminates the advantages of Internet-facilitated interaction to expand to scale the ability of diverse, and widely dispersed groups to work together to achieve a common goal. The Human Genome Project (HGP) is an unprecedented international collaborative, formally begun in October 1990 and completed in 2003.

The goal was to discover the location of all the estimated 20,000 to 25,000 human genes and make the data available to all for further biological study. The participants included the University of Santa Cruz, Whitehead Institute/MIT Center for Genome Research, Celera Genomics, Compaq's Cambridge Research Lab and Compaq, just to name a few. In total, 18 countries participated in this worldwide effort.

The data collection and analysis required collaboration of diverse computing assets in order to make available the massive computing power needed for this project. The type of computing used in the HGP is called "distributed computing." Distributed computing allows the harnessing of idle processing power of computers and shunts it into a project focused on finding solutions to complex problems. This project and its thousands of challenges and problems were solved by a widely dispersed group of computer users working together to provide input.

The interface with all parties was handled on workstations that allowed data exchanges among a wide range of computers, including large parallel computers deployed at national supercomputer centers, national laboratories, and smaller capacity computers operating at many sites. As a result of open access to this unique collaborative environment, excellent teamwork, and strategic thinking, the Human Genome Project was successfully completed.

In addition, the project was finished ahead of schedule. The Human Genome Project's success and early completion was due in large part to massive computing power and online collaboration that came together to drive the solution to one of the most complicated challenges in all of science, the deciphering of the mysteries to life itself.

So, you see, I'm not exaggerating when I say current MOLMP platforms such as "Second Life" and "World of Warcraft" have paved the way for video games to play an increasingly important role in world affairs. Technology has made us a "global village." In the world we live in today, the norm is that problems anywhere are the concerns of others everywhere, and in the future everyone can play a role in solving them.

By using video game-based technology, there is the advantage that the collaboration can be expanded to scale, and sustained by the presence of a viable business model. As Kanter stresses in her book, the suppression of dialogue and open communication is a calling card for the beginning of the end of a winning streak. As bad as the loss of dialogue is in a negative sense, there is equal impact in the positive sense because dialogue can turn a corporation or country's fortunes around.

With the expanding presence of online video games and virtual communities, there is an unprecedented opportunity for the promotion of dynamic dialogue. Dynamic dialogue promotes transparency. With transparency, issues aren't hidden by fears and prejudice. Transparency facilitates the prompt identification of problems and encourages a willingness to address problems at their conception. When used in combination with dynamic performance feedback (scoring) and immediate access to this data, one knows where one stands at all times.

Dynamic performance feedback establishes an ever-present reference point for constructive self-scrutiny. The numbers make you look in the mirror everyday. This is one of the most prominent features of video game play and design. Imagine if a society had such institutionalized transparency; issues could try to run but they could not hide. Innovation is advanced when those that would contribute have detailed, accurate information surrounding an issue of concern.

Kanter suggests that the key to fighting complacency and mounting a turnaround is dialogue powered by dynamic performance feedback, which immunizes one against denial. This leads to the establishment of personal accountability. Also, she puts forth, if we are to change or turn any situation around, one must be accountable for what has or has not been done. The buck must start and stop with individual accountability. Data is a form of communication and a form of dialogue. You are what the data says you are. When you are in possession of the truth about your performance, it isolates you as the person responsible.

Another important proposal I would like to present to you is that this video game initiative, assisted by the Internet, makes it possible to recruit many individuals from all walks of life who would normally be excluded. Diverse team members bring different perspectives that could form the foundation of an innovative breakthrough. This platform facilitates the addition of an untapped talent pool that is more likely to produce out-of-the-box innovation and leadership.

This is a defining plus-point for me. It is exciting to think of the prospect of recruiting a new legion of leaders that more accurately reflects the racial and cultural rainbow that makes up our planet. If video games can help solve the problems that stem from prejudice, then how can we turn our backs? We should, without hesitation, pursue putting the practice of universal inclusion into practice. This would send a loud and clear message. The system is willing and able to invest in anyone and everyone. In the digital age, the mothers and fathers of innovation should be culture blind and color blind. The only thing that should be important is the content of your character, the capability of your intellect, and your willingness to contribute.

This should not be viewed as a moral high ground gesture. This is a bottom line gesture. Tapping into the resources of our global population could bring people together to attack the challenge at hand with fresh voices and new tactics generated by their diverse life experiences. In video games we have an ideal culture medium to sprout initiative and put forth innovation.

Imagine if most of those who help solve huge societal challenges were already trained in collaborative competition techniques because they played games like "World of Warcraft," or "Second Life." These digital immigrants could migrate into projects or jobs and make the difference between success and failure. If this sounds familiar, it is because it is the same effect that immigration had in the history of this nation, and it is what helped define its greatness. This should also remind you of one of Kanter's key components for winning, the ability to establish and maintain an influx of new talented team members.

I hope that Rosabeth Kanter is not offended by my liberal interpretation of her thoughts put forth in her book, *Confidence*; especially its application in connecting the world of video games to the turnaround of our country. In retrospect, I have only repeated her formula. With her book, she connected a very high ground academic subject matter (the economic theory of corporate turnarounds), to a more grassroots arena beloved by the public—team sports.

In this section, I have put forth my hypothesis that another beloved popular icon (video games) possesses collateral assets that can be harnessed to establish a culture of winning, cultivate collaboration, and initiate innovation. With the help of video games, the same components mandatory for the turnaround of a sports team or corporation, can also apply to the turnaround of a nation.

Part Four

OVERCOMING THE INERTIA OF PREJUDICE

● ● ● ●

Video games have been around for a while now, and one thing has not changed. In spite of their broad public attraction, there are a significant number of people who just don't like them. Many think video games are *de facto* bad for people. They're violent and they are a waste time. Many take for face value all the negative information that has been publicized. Because of this pseudo-intellectual debris, many proudly proclaim that *they hate video games*. But, hate is a close kin to prejudice, and prejudice is universally born out of ignorance.

People who hate video games do so because they do not know the full extent of their capabilities. Therefore, whenever senseless and otherwise unexplainable catastrophic events occur, like the Columbine, Virginia Tech, and Northern Illinois University tragedies, video games are an easy target to shoot at. This chapter is meant to address the basis of those prejudices and, hopefully, provide information that helps suppress the prevailing ignorance. My wish is that some of you who think I'm nuts will at least say, "Hmmm, he's got a point there. Maybe these things (video games) can help do more than entertain and erode the mind."

CHAPTER TEN

HERE WE GO AGAIN!

Just when you think that society is making progress, the medical community suggests that video game addictive disorder should be a recognized diagnosis. This shows that we still have a long way to go. It never ceases to amaze me how individuals and groups can project a prejudice toward anything.

As a physician and scientist, I successfully completed a liberal arts education. I minored in sociology so it would seem that I should know that prejudice is part of human nature, and it should not bother me so much. Especially since I was raised in the segregated South during a time when I could not drink out of the same water fountain as others because of the color of my skin. I know that I should be acclimatized to the presence of prejudice. But whenever a preconceived, erroneous, baseless, negative predisposition toward an entity, cause or process rears its ugly head, I momentarily feel the urge to check myself in to a psychiatric hospital for the protection of others and myself.

I recently faced another medication moment when a well-meaning lady wrote me a letter in the aftermath of my groundbreaking research on how video games can train surgeons. As I mentioned earlier, my research shows that training surgeons with video games can make them faster and more accurate. The media coverage of this revelation was global, and I became dubbed the Nintendo Surgeon and the X BOX DOC. But all the reaction was not of a positive nature. The following letter is a sample of the large number of aggressive negative responses:

Dear Dr. Rosser:

I have just read an article from the Los Angeles Times about your findings that surgeons who played video games regularly performed intricate surgery better. Have you ever considered piano players? Or anyone else who practiced some kind of dexterity tasks to see if this could have an impact?

When I was a child I was forced to take piano lessons and to practice for hours a week. When I became a teenager, I was such a fast typist that a manual typewriter could not keep up with me. I believe this was all because of my piano playing. I believe that all of this is about a matter of practice with fine motor skills.

I am sorry, but I guess I'm just prejudiced and hate to see you recommending video games.

Sincerely,
Anonymous

When I first read the letter, a sickening feeling came over me. I was forced to stare the societal malignancy of prejudice in the face once again. I had flash backs to when I was a child growing up in the Mississippi Delta in the sixties and the whites terminating their daily paper subscriptions when I became the first black paper boy in my hometown of Moorhead, Mississippi. I shuddered at the memory of a city swimming pool being destroyed so people of color could not swim there. I bent my head toward the ground as I remembered how I could treat only black patients, and I had to examine them in a converted closet on my family practice rotation as a senior in medical school—in my hometown.

The pain resurfaced after all these years. Even though this situation had nothing to do with race, this demonstration of prejudice still had a profound effect. There was an uncomfortable familiarity. As Martin Luther King, Jr. once suggested, "Racism and prejudice anywhere is a threat to freedom everywhere." How do otherwise good and upstanding citizens have the audacity to pick and choose potential reservoirs of hope? This nation is in decline and we should use all the resources we can muster to turn this situation around. The fact that these assets may come in the form of video games should not make a difference.

My biggest fear is that all of this is leading to video game "profiling." Slogans such as, "The only good video game is one that hasn't been created yet." "If you play video games, you have the potential to be a mass murderer." "Video game players are fun to be around but they are not as intelligent. I will never let my child date a video game player." Where does it end? Can we envision a day when a college president will stand in the schoolhouse door and proclaim, "A video game player will come into this school over my dead body? They need their own school. We must have segregation today and segregation forever."

Of course, these are my own personal exaggerated extrapolations of video game prejudice. But, seriously, I do see crossover parables to a period in the history of this nation where misguided racial misperceptions were taken to an extreme. The evil of prejudice is that it leads to bias. Bias can then lead to false impressions that subsequently become ingrained.

Video games elicit a fear factor among people that prejudice them against assimilating positive collateral video games assets into the mainstream. A video game is not a Boogey Man lurking in the shadows of society, slowly strangling our intellectual and societal evolution. Over the years, the infiltration of prejudice toward video games, and popular culture in general, has gained a foothold. That which we do not understand, we fear. Fear can then be the fuel of catastrophic irrational behavior. In the past, it has been shown that a lack of knowledge of different cultures allows society to assign details of their own choosing. Often, these details have no bearing on the truth. As a result, vicious premeditated acts of persecution have been committed.

These negative consequences flow within the fabric of a tragic death shawl. Prejudicial societal responses lead to the adoption of policies that take decades or hundreds of years to overcome. We must not let video games become a casualty of this misguided practice.

Frankly, I would use the back of the devil's tail if it meant I could help this great nation continue to be a strong and boundless repository of hopes, dreams and accomplishments. There is a well-known story of a man having difficulty swimming in the ocean. He became very frightened and could not go on. He prayed for God to send help. A boat appeared and it was small with patches used unsuccessfully to close the many leaks, and water was slowly coming in. He waved to the captain and declined to get in. The man continued to pray and along came another boat. This boat had a sputtering engine so he waved to the captain to continue on his way.

The man continued to pray and very shortly afterwards, another boat came. The boat was a magnificent vessel but the captain was drunk. His clothing was tattered and a patch was covering a missing eye. The man refused to get in the boat and waved for it to continue on its way. Then all of the sudden, he developed intense paralytic leg cramps and shortly thereafter drowned. Well, after he died, he went to Heaven. As he stood before God, the first thing out of his mouth was, "Lord, I prayed and prayed. Why did you not help me?" God stared with a puzzled look on his face and said, "I sent three boats to rescue you but you didn't get in."

We as a society cannot make the same mistake as this misguided soul. Let us not throw back the video game life preserver. If this nation is to have a future that is as great as its past, we will have to use any and all assets to help make that wish a reality.

As I looked deeper at this issue, the letter I just shared does more than just ask a resounding question, "Why video games?" It also makes a statement, "Anything but video games!" This letter is but a snapshot of how deep the prejudice toward video games really goes. I believe that rather than consider that video games could contribute to the greater good; the person who wrote that letter would choose to turn their back on a positive resource. All because they have a personal misguided opinion about video games and their contribution to the troubles of the world that we live in.

This opinion and belief is not just limited to people like the one who wrote the letter. Some of the greatest minds and authorities in our country have echoed this narrow attitude. The book, *Everything Bad Is Good For You*, shared an opinion from famed pediatrician, Dr. Spock's most recent books on effective parenting. He stated that the best that you can say about video games is that they help to promote hand and eye coordination in children. Besides that, he thought that video games were a colossal waste of time.

When asked, most respected experts respond with a similar pre-packaged negative retort. However, their positions are not grounded in fact, but by a technique that Johnson identified as amplified selectivity. By focusing on isolated negative properties or reports, and projecting worst-case scenarios, a person is able to construct a skewed negative impression of anything. In his book, Johnson offered a creative verbal illustration of this tactic to illustrate the slight of mind shell game that amplified selectivity presents. The target of his example was a popular scared cow. Johnson centered his illustration on books.

Can anyone in their right mind construct a scenario where books are labeled as being bad for you? You would think that this would be impossible. How could you bad mouth books? But what if video games had been invented before books? How would the usefulness profile of books be interpreted? Using amplified selectivity, books would be hands-down bad for you. Under these theoretical circumstances, most would be of the opinion that reading books under-stimulates the senses and renders the reader isolated while forcing them to be slaves to a narrative that follows a fixed linear path. Books would be viewed as discriminating because persons with dyslexia could not use them.

Of course, none of us believe that books are bad. They have a multitude of positive attributes that make them outstanding vehicles for knowledge transfer and enlightenment. But Johnson's illustration shows how selective amplification can skew anything.

This debating technique has served to create damaging misconceptions that blind the general public to the upside of video games as it relates to enhancing the greater good, and more importantly, their prospect of playing a role in advancing the interests of our nation. We must change this perception, even if it means not taking the advice of experts like Dr. Spock and resisting perpetuating the opinion that society would be better served by placing all video games in a garbage disposal.

CHAPTER ELEVEN

WHY PEOPLE HATE VIDEO GAMES

In 2005, Stephen Johnson stretched the boundaries of our imagination with, *Everything Bad Is Good For You: How Today's Pop Culture Is Actually Making Us Smarter*. It was a New York Times bestseller. I've been talking about that book throughout this one because it is a rallying point around which my hypothesis about video games is anchored. In the beginning of the book, he exposes the prejudice many have about pop culture and video games in particular.

To illustrate the point, he critiques a commentary by George Will. Will is a world-renowned, award winning columnist/author and many pay attention to what he says. In the particular commentary that Johnson notes, Will expounds on the negative impact of pop culture. His piece was striking because it reads like an oration from a citizen of the Matrix oblivious to the fact that he is living the existence of a glorified test tube baby. Will asserts that the proper cadence of evolution has been forced off-step because today's generation is under siege by its addiction to graphic entertainment. He chooses to focus with great dismay on the narrowing gulf between entertainment choices of children and adults. This is what he calls the "formation of an increasingly infantilized society that is sleep walking through a dumb-down process, much like a car and its occupants traveling through an automatic car wash."

While George Will is an incredibly intelligent man, and I respect his thoughts on many subjects in which he is far more informed than I, there is a gulf of disagreement that lies between us concerning the impact of pop culture—especially video games—on the societal profile of our nation. In light of the misinformation and lack of information out there, I can understand why he has taken this position. Bias based on a lack of understanding is a common occurrence. I should know because at one time I was a technology prejudicial perpetrator.

Many of my colleagues will not believe that in the early 1980s, Butch Rosser, the futuristic surgeon and technocrat, felt that computers were part of a communist plot to destroy the United States of America. I once viewed computers as highly contagious viruses that could infiltrate our central nervous systems and incapacitate our higher brain functions by slowly taking over intellectual tasks that we would normally perform.

My theory suggested that this cyber substance abuse would insidiously give raise to a dependence on computers to perform even the most mundane intellectual task. I can hear you chuckle, but just try to remember a phone number and see what happens. I was particularly concerned about the erosive intellectual influence that it could have on our youth. I felt that the infiltration of computers into their everyday lives would lead to a nation of intellectual cripples who would eventually squander our nation's edge in ingenuity and productivity. My conspiracy theory concluded that Communism would then take over the country without firing a shot. Far in the future when historians would perform an autopsy to determine the cause of our nation's demise, the death certificate would list as the cause of death: poisoning by our own hand. The summary would read, "We regret to inform you that your nation has perished because of digitalized suicide."

The best example that justified my fears happened on a hot summer day after church when I took my family to Kentucky Fried Chicken. We entered through the drive-through window and I asked for a bucket of chicken with slaw, mashed potatoes and biscuits. The clerk repeated the order and announced that the cost was $13.95. I paused and said, "Pardon me, ma'am. But there is no way that all that food only costs $13.95. There must be some mistake."

The irritated teenager aggressively responded, "Sir, I said that will be $13.95." I then politely said, "I am sorry ma'am but that cannot be right, the math is off. Please, if you don't believe me, do the math is your head."

"Look sir," she said very annoyed, "I pushed the button on the register with the picture of the thigh, the breast and the bucket. The computer in the register says that you owe $13.95, and that is what you owe."

Realizing the utter futility of trying to reason with this "child of the walking dead," I said, "thank you" and accepted the inaccurate amount of change and took it to Baskin and Robbins and bought dessert. Believe me, I don't think that was the Christian thing to do! However, at that moment, I was reminded of a quote from Chiparopai, an old Yuma woman circa 1924, when she was asked about the impact of the white man's ways on her society. She said, "We eat the white man's food, and it makes us soft; we wear the white man's heavy clothing and it makes us weak.... Yes, we know that when you come, we die."

I made a similar connection to coming of the computer age. The Kentucky Fried Chicken incident was proof to me the digital poison had been so effective the cashier was functioning cognitively on an amebic level and did not know it. There was no hope in sight because it was clear that any and all efforts to pry that cashier from the clutches of synaptic suicide were going to be met with fierce resistance and failure. Truly the fate of our nation had already been sealed.

Obviously, at some point, my thinking changed. It happened on a day when my youngest brother, Ludie was staying with me while he was going to graduate school. One day I came home early. I put my things on the dining room table as I always do, and I heard a sound coming from his room. I kept hearing this statement in a familiar infant voice, "Got to love me, I'm the baby." It was the voice of the baby dinosaur character from a popular television show at the time called *Dinosaurs*. I kept hearing this voice say this statement over and over again. I walked into his room and I saw my first Macintosh computer. He was programming it to remind himself not to hit a certain key when doing his reports. At that moment

I was struck by an epiphany. *Computers are programmed to achieve goals dictated by us.* And it is our responsibility to program the computer properly to perform a task so that we can positively dictate our destiny. We are not just along for the ride.

Subsequently, I went on to enroll into what I call the Abraham Lincoln School of Technology. I read everything that I could on computer theory and programming. Now, as I look back over my life, I am the author of a *cadre* of computer assisted training tutorials, use robots to surgically heal, and remotely care for people in the Ecuadorian rain forest by looking at a television screen while being thousands of miles away. Today, totally self taught, most consider me a technocrat. What a transformation, eh?

My life's journey has broadened my boundaries of possibility and expanded my tolerance for the prospects for change. In contrast to Mr. Will, I am not frightened by the closure of the gap between young and old and their entertainment preferences. I see this merger of both groups as an opportunity to realize the strength of this nation. I believe that the key to progress is connected to our ability to *maintain the spirit of a terminal 12-year-old*. As a cohesive unit, both groups could hold court on the vast plains of exploration, innovation and hope. The prize will be revolutionary societal advancement. However, to get to that prize, we have to confront our preconceived notions of prejudice.

The Research Shows...

On April 20, 1999, two high school boys walked into their school and killed 12 of their fellow students, one teacher, and injured 23 others. The school, of course, was Columbine, and the media immediately began conducting a search for why these two boys would do this. Their answer: Eric Harris and Dylan Klebold had played too many violent video games. Unfortunately, this was just one of a rash of school shootings this country has endured over the last two decades, most recently the Virginia Tech tragedy in April 2007 and the Northern Illinois University shooting in February 2008.

Because of these tragic events, focus has been placed on video game research in an effort to identify the harm from video games that could befall the public. In one respect, this mimics the concern generated by television in its early days. I think today it would be fair to say that too much television or too much anything is not good for you. In the early days, television was also blamed for all kinds of doomsday scenarios. It is important to note that television research has matured and become more *fair and balanced*, and reliable studies revealed that shows like *Sesame Street* were able to provide content that is both entertaining and empowering educationally.

Video game research today is nowhere near this level of sophistication or reliability. Nevertheless, the body of work is growing and has generated controversy. The main points of contention have to do with *physical health, cognitive skills, and social and emotional well-being*. For many, the research so far overwhelmingly reflects the common perceptions of video games being bad and totally out of control.

Effects on Physical Health

While there has *not* been a reliable, comprehensive study conducted to document the effects of extended video game play on children's physical health, studies suggest that extended video and computer game play may put children at increased risk for obesity, seizures, repetitive stress injuries and eyestrain. The amount of time American children spend engaged in sedentary activities, such as watching television and playing video games, is considered by many researchers to be an important environmental factor for childhood obesity.

Obesity has been called the most common health problem facing children today and its incidence has been increasing, especially since the 1980s. To the degree that research about television viewing can be correlated to video games, a number of studies reveal that the risk for obesity increases two percent for every additional hour children spend seated in front of a television screen each day.

Beyond the risk of obesity, a number of studies have documented that playing video games may trigger epileptic seizures in some children. Ricci and Vigevano studied 12 different commercially available games and found a propensity for varying degrees of seizure activity activation. It is generally believed that rapidly flashing images activate the seizures.

As we all have been learning recently, too much time working on computers can lead to a variety of health hazards, such as eyestrain, increased myopia, and muscular and skeletal problems. Visual strain is the number one complaint of frequent computer users. Dr. Jeffrey Anschel of Corporate Vision Consulting summed it up, "We are increasingly becoming an information society, and we are paying the price with our eyesight." While most of the clinical information about these disorders refers to adults, it is reasonable to expect that heavy players could suffer from these problems, no matter what their age.

Carpal tunnel syndrome is almost a household word these days, yet there are an even wider variety of muscular and skeletal disorders associated with heavy computer and video game use, including tendonitis and nerve compression. The causes for these types of disorders vary from poor posture at the computer/video game console to the repetitive nature of movements used with input devices (such as the keyboard, mouse and joysticks). Once again, most of the information on these types of disorders has been collected on adults. However, video game detractors would suggest the earlier the offending behavior or activity begins, it stands to reason the sooner and more aggressive deleterious consequences will play out in adult life.

Lately, these types of studies have begun focusing on children. In March 2000, Nintendo of America, a major video game manufacturer, acknowledged that physical problems could occur when playing video games on their consoles. Because of this finding, they agreed to supply protective gloves to approximately 1.2 million children because of numerous reports of hand injuries caused by the control stick of a particular game. Excessive video game playing has also led to documented cases of a form of tendonitis dubbed "Nintendinitis," caused by repeatedly pressing buttons with the thumb during game play. This was preceded even earlier by a condition called "Pac Man Thumb" syndrome.

Effects on Cognitive Skills

A growing number of studies are finding a negative correlation between the amount of time spent playing video games and school performance. Some early studies showed an inconsistent relationship between video game play and grades. More recently, a preponderance of studies are claiming a fairly consistent negative correlation between recreational video game play and school performance. Harris and Williams showed that high school students who reported extensive play and those who reported spending more money on video games received lower grades in English classes. Others have documented a similar relationship between amount of play and grades for college students.

One thought-provoking theory as to why heavy video game use correlates with poor school performance, has been called the *displacement hypothesis*—electronic media are hypothesized to influence both learning and social behavior by taking the place of activities such as reading, family interaction, and social play with peers. Simply put, whatever time children spend on electronic entertainment media is not being spent on other educational and social activities.

In a sample of eighth and ninth grade students, the average boy plays video games for 13 hours a week. According to the theory, this translates into 13 hours each week that he is not engaged in homework, reading, or participating in other activities. Researchers now show that one out of five boys play at least 19 hours (or about three-quarters of a day) a week. And one in 10 plays for at least 27 hours a week—more than a full day. It is of great concern that those students who play this much, put themselves at greater risk for school failure because they are not using this time to do school work.

Effects on Social and Emotional Well-Being

In these areas, once again, many opponents to video games choose to borrow from what we have learned from research on the effect of television, which has shown that both the amount of television watched and the content of the shows can have substantial effects on children. Regarding amount, research has shown that heavy television viewers expend less effort at schoolwork, play less well with friends, and have fewer hobbies and activities than light viewers.

Content also has effects that are independent of the amount of exposure. For example, television programs high in violence have been shown to increase aggression and fear. They desensitize young viewers to violence and increase their appetites for more violence. On the other side of the coin, educational television has been shown to teach pro-social attitudes (i.e. non-racist attitudes), skills and empathy.

While the research conducted on video games is still growing, many opponents feel that there are at least four reasons why we should be prepared for the possibility that video games will have an even greater impact than television. These reasons are based on what we already know from both educational research and research on television effects. They are: (1) Identification with an aggressor increases imitation of the aggressor; (2) Active participation increases learning; (3) Repetition increases learning; and (4) Rewards increase learning (It is ironic that these strengths of video games are ignored when it comes to the education argument).

The research on the effects of violent games conducted thus far strongly suggests a reason for concern about the connection between video game play and anti-social behavior. Anderson and Bushman conducted a meta-analysis of 35 different studies of violent video games to see if they reveal patterns in their findings. They identified a consistent pattern in five areas:

1. Exposure to violent games increases physiological arousal.

2. Exposure to violent games increases aggressive thoughts.

3. Exposure to violent games increases aggressive emotions.

4. Exposure to violent games increases aggressive actions.

5. Exposure to violent games decreases positive pro-social (i.e., helping) actions.

Based on all the evidence presented so far, why send the jury out for deliberations? Video games are hands down guilty as charged. They are a menace to society. No wonder they are the targets that the public loves to hate. But hold on just a minute. Any credible system of justice allows for, and demands that both sides of the story be told before passing judgment.

The other side to this story...

Those who are card-carrying video game bashers should be very cautious when embracing negative video game studies because when these studies are critically reviewed, problems with the external validity are uncovered. Frequently, the investigational reproduction demands are so arduous that it is difficult to get reliable data outside the original investigators. In other words, other investigators cannot verify the research. This is a sign that any conclusions rendered by this study may not be correct. Another problem is the way some studies are designed. Many promote inherent participant suspicion and bias, which is difficult to eliminate. This results in methodology compliance issues. And if the participants do not follow the rules of the studies, the results cannot be viewed as being reliable.

Another issue with many of the negative studies is that they are often without statistical analysis. And when an analysis is done, it is usually of the correlation-only variety. A correlation-only study can breed inaccurate conclusions. Not all correlation studies are of low statistical or academic power. But, to be taken seriously, it has to be supported by a cadre of statistics to be considered noteworthy. Remember, correlation is not causation without other evaluation parameters giving statistical support.

Unfortunately, violence and aggression studies with video games have produced monumental misguided conclusions. This results from investigators using arousal-based measurement parameters to account for all video game effects on aggressive behavior. If this data were collected while playing football, baseball or soccer, similar findings could be found. Should we ban all of these activities? Another fact that is frequently overlooked when debating the violence and video game issue is that there are absolutely no high power studies linking violent video game play to actual aggression.

Video game opponents do not elaborate on this consideration when they are making their arguments. Something I ask them to consider is that even with worst-case scenarios, violent media affects only a few individuals who often already have issues with violence and aggressive behavior. How can we place all of society's ills on the back of video games?

The parade of "weak links" in frequently quoted negative video game studies is seemingly limitless. Some studies use "violent" and "nonviolent" games that are not significantly different in violent content. This is a major breach in study design. In some studies, two groups are supposedly exposed to two different stimuli but after closer scrutiny they are really the same. Future studies need to do a better job of assessing the violent content of the video games being compared. Also, some studies have used a "control" or "nonviolent game" title that was more boring, annoying or frustrating than the violent game. You don't have to have an advanced degree to understand the shortcomings of these studies. The obvious solution for future studies is to do more pilot testing or manipulation checks on such aggression-relevant study design. And so far, that type of investigative effort is not the standard.

Another one of the most serious challenges to the integrity of most of these studies is unrepresentative participant sampling. They don't have enough people in the study to allow the data to be deemed reliable. My assessment must also point out that some of these studies did not report sufficient data to enable calculations of an effect size for participants who actually played a video game. You do not know who did what. This is an issue in several frequently quoted studies in which half of the participants played a video game, while the other half merely observed. Future reports should include the individual data being given. This is the approach that I took in my video game and surgical skill study.

Some studies that reportedly studied aggressive behavior have measured variables that are not true aggressive behavior. This tends to lump things together and give a higher and inaccurate measurement of aggression. I call this "juicing" the numbers. Some of the studies have used trait or personality aggression scales as measures of aggressive behavior in short-term experiments. This is not acceptable because there is no way that a short-term exposure to violent versus nonviolent video games (e.g., 20 minutes) can account for one's past demonstration of aggression.

In this short-term context, any aggressive traits found might possibly be conceived as a measure of cognitive priming by the design of the study. In plain English, the aggressive traits observed were prepped to occur. Clearly, this type of study design will skew any effort to accurately measure aggressive behavior. A related problem is that some studies have included hitting an inanimate object as a measure of aggressive behavior. Most modern definitions of aggression restrict its application to behaviors that are intended to harm another person. The obvious solution for future studies is to use better ways to measure aggression.

Probably the most compelling reason to *slow our roll* on passing judgment on the negative impact of video games is the fact that there are no great longitudinal studies. Thus, one must rely on longitudinal studies in the TV/movie domain to get a reasonable guess as to the likely long-term effects. *Guesses that are promoted by individuals to represent facts are just not welcome in the scientific arena.* Hopefully in the future, major funding and more researchers will enter this fertile field of scientific investigation and help settle this conflict once and for all.

CHAPTER TWELVE
CURING THE CURSE OF PREJUDICE: EXTOLLING THE GOOD OF VIDEO GAMES

For those of us who can see the potential of video games to contribute to society in a positive way, winning the battle for legitimacy should be our main focus. However, as I have previously stated, this is difficult due to the ignorance surrounding video games and the fact that many titles are not of high ground substance. Games like *Grand Theft Auto* make it difficult to make a positive case for video games. They are seen as frivolous items that result in only foolhardy, mindless activity. For many years, the station of video games on the "recognition of worth" food chain has been on the amebic level. They are suffering from an extreme case of lack of public and self esteem.

Unfortunately, the general public and the current industry brain trust are suffering from the same disease. Both do not recognize the full potential video games have to contribute positively to society. Both factions exert feeble organized effort to explore this possibility. The public has focused on the ability of video games to provide entertainment and the industry has focused on their ability to make money.

How do video games emerge from the shadow of prejudice? How do they receive recognition for having qualities that could help mankind? You do it by showcasing the good that goes unnoticed. I am a cup half-full kind of guy. Therefore, I will now discuss the research that identifies the positive effects of video games. The awareness of their contributory assets establishes a foundation with which a constructive agenda can be formulated. Remember, an empty wagon makes all the noise. I would like to now fill the wagon with facts about the good in video games, and hopefully silence misguided critics and recruit them to become allies to a revolution.

It would not be considered radical thought to assume that everyone in this country has gotten onboard the *technology train,* and our citizens enjoy the highest possible level of computer literacy. But this could not be further from the truth. There is a *digital divide* that has now grown into a *digital abyss* as far as computer literacy is concerned. Strategic members of our society still have sub par exposure, and participation with use of computers. For many, video games offer a *first contact* introduction to computer technology. Playing video games helps to foster a comfort level with computers, computer interfaces, input/output devices, and technology as a whole.

It is true that it is not unusual for children as young as age three to be aware and comfortable with terms such as point and click. But you should not assume that this is the norm. It is sad to say, but many children still do not have computers in their homes or schools. Video game consoles are more ubiquitous and cost-effective. Therefore, they can offer easy access. A great asset if you want to accomplish expansion of scale of computer literacy. With more and more adults engaging in video games, a similar purpose for adults could be served as well.

Some have suggested that video games are training wheels that set the stage for computer literacy. This is something that should not be taken lightly. Today, jobs on the most non-technical level are frequently based around competence with this skill set. Have you noticed your UPS or FedEx delivery team lately and the devices in their hands? Who's next, the Pizza Hut delivery guy? Don't laugh! You can run, but you can't hide. These skills are needed in everything we do.

Spatial and visual attention skill sets are influenced by video games. One study designed to determine participants' relative ability to keep track of several different things on a computer screen at the same time (a skill similar to those needed by flight controllers), concluded that expert video game players were better at maintaining divided visual attention than novices.

In a second study, after five hours of playing a video game, all participants showed increased response speed in a visual attention task, regardless of previous experience, thus demonstrating a causal relationship between video game play and visual attention skills. This also suggests that warming up with video games can help with performance. As more and more imagery technology crosses over to the civilian experience, the public will need to incorporate these skill sets more and more into their jobs. For instance, the tragedy of 9-11 has stimulated a massive influx of imagery technology, and the surveillance and security arena is a hot bed of expansion that will need qualified workers.

Another research-proven feature of playing video games includes their ability to improve fine motor skills. In the past, this has been only a concern for child developmental psychologists, competitive athletes or rehabilitation therapists. Because of the proliferation of computers in the workplace, the ability to adeptly interface and complete tasks with console and handheld technology is a skill set which is becoming a standard requirement for jobs in all walks of life.

The military is demanding that this be a primary skill set for all service men and women. No matter what your job is in the military, at some time you will need to exhibit superior fine motor skills. Video games can provide opportunities for preparation and practice in order to establish, and maintain those skills. Better eye/hand coordination is another positive result of video game play. Early studies of video games tested subjects on a task and compared the task performance outcomes with survey results of video game play. In one study comparing 31 video game users (both home and arcade) and 31 non-users (all college students), users had significantly better eye-hand coordination.

An abundance of evidence suggests that video games can help improve the reaction to various stimuli. One study tested a group of 46 Japanese boys and girls in kindergarten (4-6 years old) divided into players and non-players. The study was designed to assess the relation between past gaming and parallel-processing skills, to which there was not a significant difference between groups. However, they did note that reaction times in the players were significantly faster than that of the non-players. Thus, it is possible that practice on video games could improve information-processing skills.

Increased spatial visualization skills (the ability to interpret positions of objects as related to their occupation of a specified space) have long been suggested as a haven of influence for video games. In a study involving 47 third graders (24 boys and 23 girls), the relation between video games and spatial visualization ability was tested. The experimental group outperformed the control group in spatial visualization skills. Perhaps more importantly, children with initial poor performance were able to improve their spatial visualization skills after playing video games requiring those same skills.

This finding was replicated in a study of 70 undergraduate students without any previous video game experience. Participants were given a pre-test and a post-test in spatial relations of designated objects, between which the experimental group was subjected to eight sessions of video game play. The experimental group significantly outperformed the control group, supporting the hypothesis that spatial visualization can be improved by video game playing.

Increased visual attention skills are becoming more of a pre-requisite skill set as our society and workplace continues to increase its imagery technology density. An article in the journal *Nature* hinted at a possibility that video game play could increase competence in this area. The researchers performed several experiments aimed at determining if video gaming could enhance the capacity of visual attention (e.g., increased ability to process information over time and an increase in the number of visual items that can be tracked) and its spatial distribution (e.g., enhanced allocation of spatial attention over the visual field). They found a positive correlation between video gaming and visual attention processing. And non-video gamers were able to increase their visual attention skills with just one hour of practice per day on games that required visual attention after a 10-day trial.

By contrast, the control group, who played one hour of games with a different format and design (e.g., rotational skills involving attention to an individual item), did not improve their visual attention processing. This suggests that video games can improve a deficient skill set. Furthermore, all video games are not created equal and video games, and indiscriminant play does not produce the same positive results. These studies also opened the door to the possibility that warm-up with over the counter video games, could be beneficial in improving task execution.

A fact not generally appreciated is that effective skill transfer can be achieved even though some video games do not provide perceptive references for movements (i.e., force feedback). The brain readily compensates by using substitutive visual clues as reference points to make decisions. There is one rule as it relates to the human brain, what the environment does not give; the brain will create the data points needed to assist in the execution of a task. Therefore sophisticated and costly training platforms may not be needed to transfer skill. A video game console may be all the technology necessary for many types of education and training needs.

One of the most exciting positive attributes of video games is their ability to increase task performance by using virtual reality simulations. Video games that allow interaction with reality based situations (simulator or experiential training) can lead to acquisition of complex, real-world skills such as driving, flying airplanes, playing golf and even surgery. My 11-year-old twin daughters, Taylor and Tianna are learning how to drive by using the video game *Grand Turismo*. They have all the proper mechanical interfaces such as steering wheels, brakes, throttle and gear shifter. Initially, they did not like to shift the gears.

But I insisted and told them that if they wanted to drive my cars when they got older, they would have to drive a stick shift. After an initial learning curve, they loved it and are now very competent and competitive with Daddy. We drive the simulated track at Nuremberg with similar performance profiles, and they are only 11 years of age. This is the power of simulation. Imagine if all of our children could have video games help develop competent and safe driving skills. This is not a dream but a reality ready to be grasped.

The impact of video game and simulator training has been most evident in the arena of the military and aerospace communities. Jimmy Doolittle started it all by inventing the first airplane simulator. He converted a toy airplane from a carnival ride and used it to train pilots to fly while relying on their instrument in difficult weather and at night. Aviation accidents caused by landing at night and in bad weather decreased by 90 percent after the first year.

Since that time, simulator techniques have become standard training practice in the military and civilian aerospace communities. The Army has recognized the benefits of video games for teaching skills and has licensed the popular violent video game series *Rainbow Six* to train their special operations forces because it is an excellent way to teach all of the steps necessary to plan and conduct successful operations.

The biggest military vote of confidence in video games was the development of its own representative video game called *America's Army*. This was developed as an effort to attract recruits by gaining proximity using what interests them and also to evaluate the embracing of video games into the military's cultural mainstream. From all accounts, it has been well received by military leadership and recruits alike. Video games will have an increasing role in the preparation of tomorrow's warriors. With the advent of more and more robots and unmanned vehicles on the battlefield, video games stand to have an expanding influence on how wars will be fought and won in the future.

So far, I have pointed out video game attributes that help to mature hand/eye coordination and the execution of manual tasks. I would warn you to avoid the trap of limiting the extent of the positive attributes of video game play to only being applicable to manual task enhancements. Video games offer an abundance of positive attributes for applications in learning and decision-making.

Investigators have identified facets of video game play that can be parlayed into promoting a superior learning experience. Video game developers have instinctively implanted best practice collateral learning assets into the game play of their titles. Unfortunately, frontline educators are lagging in grassroots implementation. At a recent Federation of Scientists Summit, features of games and simulations that could be applied to improve education and training were discussed. Some of the positive video game attributes for learning included the following:

Clear learning goals: In a good game, goals are clear; you know why you are learning something and there are opportunities to immediately apply what you learn.

Broad experiences and practice opportunities are presented that continue to challenge the learner and reinforce expertise: In games and simulations, learners are presented with a broad set of experiences and practice opportunities—you can operate powerful equipment or fly through the interior of a cell—learning from a world that has color, complexity, and challenge, rather than a set of abstract facts devoid of real-world context. Additionally, the "lesson" can be practiced over and over again until mastered.

With continuous monitoring of progress, and use of this information to diagnose performance and adjust instruction, the learner gains a level of mastery: Games continually monitor the metrics of play and the player's progress, and feedback is clear and often immediate. A good game moves at a rate that keeps the player at the edge of his or her capabilities, moving to higher challenges as mastery is acquired.

Encouragement of inquiry and formulation of answers gives the learner information within real-world context: Compelling games often motivate their players to seek out information on game strategies and concepts from other gamers, friends, tip guides, Websites, and other resources. All of this activity requires good old fashion reading.

Contextual Bridging: Games and simulations can close the gap between what is learned and putting what is learned to use. Video games eliminate the age-old question from students, "Why do I need to know this?" For example, one can learn theories of the business management of an NFL football franchise—supply, demand, pricing and budget—but the retained facts concerning these subjects come alive in the "owners mode" of a popular video game as players manage an NFL football franchise.

Time on Task: The ability to hold the attention of players is a hallmark of modern video and computer games (time-on-task). Some game players spend hundreds of hours mastering games. Game designers understand how to keep an audience engaged, while delivering critical information for attaining the game's objectives.

Motivation and Strong Goal Orientation: Games also have features that are highly motivating; that is, game players continue to play games, *even after failure*, to get better at them. This is an attribute that could contribute significantly in the teaching and learning of difficult and complex material.

Scaffolding: Games and simulations can offer scaffolding to facilitate a *building block* learning method. Scaffolding provides learners with cues, prompts, hints and partial solutions to keep them progressing through learning, until they are capable of directing and controlling their own learning path.

Personalization: There is significant interest in how technology can be used to tailor learning to the individual. Schools are starting to look at adapting material to the student, rather than exposing them to rigid, non-optimal lesson plans. Video games and simulations can offer educational experiences in a format that will appeal to all learners, regardless of their style of learning.

Infinite Patience: Another feature of video games and simulations valuable for learning is that learning can go on with the game, expressing infinite patience. Even the most dedicated teachers can lose patience with a difficult student. Also to be considered is the danger that a teacher may conclude a student "just isn't cut out for math," and give up on them all together.

In addition, a teacher's impatience may intimidate a learner, or influence how learners perceive themselves. It is more difficult to gain the trust of a student if a teacher has the belief that the student is a failure. The advantage of teaching techniques assisted by computer and video game console tutorials is that they don't lose patience. They are not judgmental and offer learners innumerable opportunities to "just try and try again."

The collateral learning assets of video games I just presented are characteristics desired by any successful lesson plan or curriculum. Along with attributes such as *probing, telescoping, and engaged consequentiality*, there is the prospect of designing an upgraded education system appropriate for the times and a *perfect learning storm*. Once a storm hits, it will engulf a new generation of learners in a best practice knowledge transfer tornado.

An asset not appreciated by those who are allies and opponents of video games, is the tremendous opportunity that playing these games offers for *family bonding*. In the face of all the forces of separation facing families today, video games provide an excellent opportunity for parents and their children to sit together and enjoy a common pastime. It helps to reinforce the family bond. With all five of my children, video games have been a source of family fun. This is the case to this day, whether at home or at the arcade.

When I visit my older children, we always find an arcade and go have a ball. During the course of the outing, there are items of individual and family importance that come out as a by-product. There is just something about seeing your parent having fun with a joystick in their hands that removes barriers that otherwise could be an obstacle to communication. On the other hand, the elation of beating dad or mom in grand prix racing can sometimes earn an opportunity for a parent to talk to their child about something that has become an issue, but, for whatever reason, had previously been awkward to discuss.

In closing, it is true that I am a *video game techno super freak*. But I am also a man of science and a parent. Therefore, the presence of such an avalanche of supportive data about the good of video games is welcomed and very reassuring when considering the legitimacy of the claim that video games can help society. As I ponder all the assets of video games, the most exciting part is a video game's ability to help me to be a better parent. I am a daddy who not only enjoys my children, but my children enjoy me. And video games have provided fertile common ground for that relationship to continue growing.

Part Five

THE KEY TO VICTORY: TRANSFORMING OUR EDUCATION AND TRAINING MODEL INTO AN EMPOWERMENT ECOSYSTEM

● ● ● ●

The pivotal battle for the survival of America will not be fought in foreign lands against nations or terrorists that mean us harm. Rather, it will be fought on a domestic battlefield that had previously been strategic in our rise to global prominence. Education and training is our modern day Gettysburg. Our once proud educational system needs to step up in the worst way, but its current configuration will not be able to answer the bell. Change is needed immediately, if we are to meet the challenge of global competition.

When I talk to people about the revolution that I am proposing, they think in terms of a *"killa app"* software Messiah that will descend from heaven to make what is wrong, right. Many expect a rapture to occur in the blink of an eye that will remove the stain of our failing system and put in place a learning Shangri-la. No such miracle is forthcoming. No one item will evoke true change.

We must surround our citizens with a new learning and empowerment *ecosystem*. An ecosystem represents a localized group of interdependent organisms coexisting in an environment that they both inhabit and depend on for the survival of all. Video game technology, tactics and techniques coordinated with initiatives from parents, educators, business, medicine and faith will be pivotal in establishing a revolutionary nurturing habitat, which will forge a successful and prosperous future for our nation.

CHAPTER THIRTEEN
PARENTS, IT'S ALL ABOUT YOU

Just like many American families, my family and I love to eat out on Friday nights. It does not make a difference where we go, as long as mommy or daddy do not have to cook and the family can just sit down and talk about our week and "let our hair down." I am going to share with you an incident on one of those Friday nights greatly troubled me.

It all started innocently enough. We had just finished placing our orders for food and I was laughing at something really kooky that my daughters Tianna and Taylor had just said. I then noticed another family coming in to be seated. Yes, there were a lot of families in this restaurant, but this family stood out and drew my attention.

They projected a startling portrait of the American family in the digital age. There was dad, mom, sister and brother and they all were engaged with a digital appendage. Dad and mom were talking on the cell phone, the daughter was at play with a Nintendo DS, and the son had a Sony PSP. The picture I saw stuck with me like an insect on flypaper.

I tried to turn away and get back into the spirit of my evening, but the image of this family continued to haunt me. What was wrong with this picture? A few minutes passed and I just glanced over to their table and they all were still at it. Each one of them was engrossed in their own personal *digi-sphere*. No one was talking to the other. The server brought water over for everyone and no one looked up to say thank you. Again, I was troubled. And I asked myself once more, "What is wrong with this picture?"

I tried to put this behind me and I turned to my family and began to do my usual stand up comic routine and I got my crew laughing. All of a sudden, my futile attempt to get my comedic career off the ground was interrupted by loud voices coming from *the table*. When I looked over, the little boy had put down his PSP and was trying to get his mother's attention because he wanted to tell her something important about his day.

The mom was on the phone and showed no signs of hanging up. She looked like the corporate type trying to finish up with some business loose ends. On the child's third attempt, without saying a word and without breaking the stride of her conversation, she picked up his PSP and shoved it in his direction. He reluctantly went back to playing and re-entered his play zone. I put my head down and stared at the floor because my heart became acutely very heavy. I felt so sad, for both the parent and the child. They both were missing out on an opportunity to connect, to engage in dialogue. And I knew that opportunities like that are very few and precious in today's society of two income families. This served as a wake up call for me to make sure that I took care of my business, and I went back to acting silly with my family.

A short time passed and all of a sudden I heard an angry loud voice, "Billy put that darn video game down, we are about to eat." As I looked back at *the table*, I could not help but ask myself the question once again, "What is wrong with this picture?" Dad was now scolding the child for playing with his digital companion. The same appliance that mom had used as an electronic babysitter just minutes ago. At the same time, he had a call on hold on his cell phone, mom was busy sending a text to somebody, and his sister was taking care of her new virtual puppy on her DS. What a hornet's nest of mixed signals. If the child was not confused, I was.

I am confident that it does not take a great deal of effort for you to recall your own examples of these types of scenarios. But here are a few more to try on for size: An eight-year old boy and his family are getting ready to go to church on Sunday morning and chaos and bad words erupt because he refuses to get in the car. He cannot find his Game Boy and he's not leaving without it.

Here's another: A mother in the Toys 'R Us is totally embarrassed by her 10-year-old daughter because she won't stop screaming until mom buys her a new DS. The daughter already has two, and wants another one because there is a hot new color available. And finally, the case of the parents that have to seek an emergency family counseling session because the 12-year-old son stays up until two in the morning during the school week playing "World of Warcraft." Then, the child tore up the house when his parents took his computer and the police had to intervene. All of these circumstances I just shared are cases of what I call, *game rage*. Who is at fault here, the parents or the children?

Children are not the only ones to exhibit signs and symptoms of *game rage*. A friend of mine has an adult daughter who has always loved video games, and like many of us, she has continued to play into adulthood. Her thing right now is cell phone games. She is especially captivated by a social simulation game that requires her to raise fish. It was not unusual for her to give the phone to her six-year-old daughter and let her play while she was multitasking with something else.

On this occasion, Mom was on the way to her mother's house when she gave her daughter the phone to play games while traveling. When the daughter got the phone she said, "Mom your game account is low." Mom acknowledged that she had been playing quite a bit, and she would have to replenish the account. There was nothing else said and silence ruled the interior of the vehicle. Suddenly, the daughter excitedly yelled, "Look mom what I did!" Mom took the phone and looked. Lo and behold her account had now been replenished. She instinctively showered her daughter with kudos and praises, until she let loose a shriek that would remind you of a scream from *Scary Movie 4*.

"Oh my God!" she said, "Look what you did!" The child was obviously startled by the sudden change of demeanor. "What do you mean mommy? I got you more play time." "Yes, you got me more play time," she sharply retorted, "but you started the game over. Do you know it took me over 200 hours to raise those fish?" This mother, who 30 seconds earlier, was lovingly praising her six-year-old daughter for her initiative, had now turned into a South Park mommy from hell scolding her child for killing her virtual fish. This otherwise loving, caring wonderful mother became the victim of temporary insanity. All of this was caused by the death of some virtual fish!

Who is at fault for this kind of behavior illustrated in the previous stories? Is it the child or the parent? Are these situations occurring because of the child's lack of moral fiber? It is apparent who is at fault here. I place the responsibility for this type of inappropriate behavior squarely on the parents. I face parents all the time that relate similar stories and they claim that they don't know how their children fell into such undesirable behavior patterns.

Are you kidding me? Of course many don't like the answer I give. I tell them, all they have to do is look in the mirror and they will find the architect of the child from hell. You! The $64,000 question is why do they seem unaware of the connection between the lack of parental leadership and how it plays a role in their children's behavior outside of the home; especially at school? The lack of a proper parental cadence toward academic endeavors is a major factor in a child's poor performance in the classroom.

Parenting is a very tough challenge and one that we cannot be successful at all the time. It is not the place for a person with a delicate ego. Similar to baseball, there is no way to always bat a thousand. But just as you don't have to bat a thousand to get in the baseball hall of fame, you don't have to bat a thousand to get into the parents hall of fame. But you do have to be a good, consistent performer. If you are not a good and consistent parent, it ultimately will be translated into less than optimum outcome for your child.

When bad behavior surfaces, it is a natural response for parents to take it as a personal failure, and each of us may respond to imperfection very differently. Many may use this as a wake up call to be more vigilant in their parenting responsibilities. However, a significant number will respond by shifting the blame for the child's behavior to some other target.

This reaction should come as no surprise. When facing danger, humans can be counted on to circle the wagons and go into a protective mode. It is a well-known fact that all species of the animal kingdom have an instinctive tendency to protect their young, and protect themselves. When facing this situation, many parents will draw lines in the sand.

Supposedly, these lines are drawn to protect the children from outside dangers. But the truth is that these lines are drawn to discount feelings of parental failure because the child's behavior has become an issue for public scrutiny. For those parents who blame shift, every possible cause of the problem is acknowledged, but they are reluctant to point the finger at themselves.

Let's look at some examples of this type of parental behavior. What do many parents say when their child hits another child at school? Why is the other kid out of control? When a child comes home with poor grades, why do some parents rant about how the teaching profession has gone down the drain? When a child is sent home for the chronic use of bad language and bullying in class, why do some parents quickly conclude that their child is the victim of cruel and pointless persecution?

It is not a rare occurrence to see parents ready, willing and able to blame everybody else for their children's struggles. But at the same time, do we question the lack of quality time that we spend with our kids? Do we listen when they try to tell us about their day? Do we properly address the five-year-old falling to the floor screaming in the middle of the grocery store because he or she can't have a box of Froot Loops? Where is the outcry for us to not just protect our children, but also parent our children?

Recently I became enamored with a show called *Sleeper Cell*. This show is a very detail-oriented portrayal about the tactics and operational patterns of terrorists and the law enforcement agencies that seek to thwart them. An interesting twist to the show is that the terrorists do not follow stereotypical characterizations. One of the terrorists is a blond, blue-eyed, all-American California boy who had a life-long problem with authority. He came from an upper middle class home. His mother was a professor at Berkeley and his father, a prominent businessman. He revealed that at one time he had joined the Army just to piss his liberal parents off.

Near the end of the show's season, the inevitable execution of the terrorist mission was at hand. Before the operation began, all the terrorists videotaped their final statements to the world. This young man began by thanking his parents. But it was not for the usual things that you might think. He said that he would like to thank his mom and dad for failing so miserably as parents that he was forced to escape the coddled mediocrity of America and find a noble and spiritual purpose as a holy soldier of God.

In the end, he died a victim of his own hand when the FBI foiled the cell's plans. Before he detonated a bomb strapped to his chest, he called his mom and calmly spoke to her. This was a last act of defiance and rebellion. He made her a witness to his death and clearly assigned a footnote of blame to she and his father. She responded by calling a news conference to announce that she was grieving for the death of her son and for her country as well. Because of the hand our government's policies had in the tragic loss of her son, she declared that she and her husband would be filing suit for their pain and suffering. The lawsuit was to be directed against the Pentagon that wrongly persecuted her son during his short stay in the military, and against the White House where these horrible policies originated.

Of course, let's keep this in perspective; this was a theatrical representation of a storyline that was meant to grasp the attention of the viewer for monetary gain. But, it does provide a vivid illustration of how parents struggle to accept blame for a child with a bad outcome. It takes a hell of a person to publicly admit to the world that they failed at one of the most sacred, defining duties that an individual has to shoulder.

The over the top legal reaction from the parent of the misguided individual in the show is not just limited to television and cinema. Look at the video game legal backlash that happened after Columbine and other similar incidents. As a result of the shooting, the families of the victims filed a total of nine lawsuits against the school. The courts dismissed all of them. The ruling was a strong suggestion to all parents that video games cannot carry the entire burden for this tragedy.

We need to concentrate on other factors to seek answers and one of them is effective parenting. The bottom line is that we are responsible for our children's behavior. We must actively guide them during their early years. The battle for your child to become a good citizen starts the day they are born, not the day the police calls you to come down and bail them out of jail.

Some of you may not believe that this is a fair statement with all the outside influences (from things like video games) that can sway your child. I should not have to tell you this, but many have to be reminded to accept raising your child as your primary responsibility. I agree with Ben Carson, the famous Johns Hopkins neurosurgeon. In his book *The Big Picture*, he asserts that parenting and raising a child is life's most important responsibility. He also says it is tougher than brain surgery, and I agree with him.

I have five and I have the battle scars to prove it. I am not complaining because it is my job! And I take my job very seriously.

No matter what the circumstances are, this post cannot be abandoned when the going gets a little rough; especially during these times when the future of our children and our nation hangs in the balance. The revolution that I have called you to join is primarily an education revolution and involves the destinies of all of our children. The upgrades to our education system will hold the key to our nation continuing to thrive in the future. However, no measures will make a difference if parents are not willing to be parents and lead the way.

Parental Rules of Engagement for Video Game Play

As a parent, when trying to control and harness the power of video games, you truly have a tiger by the tail. As I have explained earlier, the upside can be immense, but the downside can be cataclysmic.

Many parents fear the impact that video games will have on their children's future. They feel as if they are witnessing a runaway freight train speeding toward their children who are tied to the railroad tracks with the power cords from video game consoles. To save the child, the margin of error can be very small and have life long consequences. Most of us face the challenge of throttling our children's exposure to video games and video game play.

I would like to give my suggestions for navigating this slippery slope. There are many sources that give strategies that can be used to modulate video game play in our children. One source that makes a lot of sense and gives robust details is the one given by the Parent Teacher Association (PTA):

PTA Helpful Tips for Parents and Video Game Play

- *Check the ratings*. The Entertainment Software Rating Board (ESRB) created a system for rating video games. Use both ESRB rating symbols and content descriptors to select appropriate games for your children. Before you go shopping, visit ESRB for specific ratings information.

- *Consider your child's personality, maturity and abilities*. Remember, video game ratings only provide rough guidance. To fine tune making an accurate decision on titles, parents should consider the make-up of the child to decide which games are appropriate for them.

- *Don't stop at the ratings*. Speak to older children and other parents, rent before purchasing, read game reviews, and try out demos of games online or in stores where games are sold.

- *Look closely at the box the game comes in.* Most video games have screen shots of the game on the back of the box showing typical scenes from the game. Determine if you are comfortable with the characters, scene depiction, and level of action portrayed before you buy or rent the game. Additional screen shots are available online at game preview Websites for stores such as Game Revolution, GameStop, or GameSpy.

- *Know the store's return policy.* Many stores will not accept video game returns if the cellophane wrapping has been opened. Check with the store before you make your purchase. Many major retailers will, however, allow parents to return or exchange games sold to their children in violation of store enforcement policies regarding the sale of mature-rated video games.

- *Play video games with your children.* Playing or observing helps you understand your child's video game experience, while providing a fun parent/child activity. Talk to your child and ask him or her about the game; what makes it fun for them? What is the story line? Is the game real or make-believe?

- *Use parental controls.* Newer video game systems allow parents to restrict specific game content by rating. Check with the manufacturer of your video game system for more information, or ask a video game retail sales associate about the availability of parental controls.

- *Be cautious with "online-enabled" games.* Many popular games can be played with friends (and strangers) over the Internet. Often, these games contain live chat or other user-generated content that is not rated by the ESRB and may not be consistent with the rating assigned to the game.

- *Be aware of "mods" that can change a game.* Downloadable modification programs ("mods") can alter game content, allow unmonitored live communications and change the game's age-appropriateness. Additionally, mods can unknowingly render your child exposed to dangerous predators.

- *Set household media use rules*. Establish rules for your children and encourage open communication about their media use so they recognize what you feel is inappropriate content.

In plotting my own road map, I used a mixture of my take on the PTA suggestions and my own life experiences of being a video gamer and a parent of five. They are as follows:

Rosser's Rules and Parental Guides for Video Game Play:

1. *You Are The Quarterback Of This Game*

2. *You Must Become A Terminal 12-year-old*

3. *Know Your Child First*

4. *Be Willing To Go Back To School*

5. *Look At The Ratings With A Jaundiced Eye*

6. *Time and Place Makes A Difference*

7. *Let The Children Help Make The Rules*

8. *Consequences Are A Fact of Life*

9. *The Family That Plays Together Stays Together*

10. *Parents Must Become A Band of Brothers*

1. You Are the Quarterback of This Game

This is the first and most important rule. As the parent, you are the person responsible and you are in control. The only way you lose control as a parent is to give it up. You have to have the heart of a tiger—Tiger Woods that is.

On the last day of the 2007 PGA championship, Tiger Woods entered the competition with a comfortable lead over the field. Before tee off, the media had already started an all too familiar Tiger coronation. This was going to be his 13th major victory, only five shy of the legendary Jack

Nicholas's 18. About midway through the match, two great golfers made a run at Tiger's lead and at one point he could have fallen into a tie for first place. His opponents were not able to capitalize and Tiger went on to cruise to a two shot lead and his 13th major championship.

When asked by a reporter what went through his mind when he was about to be overtaken and possibly have the championship slip away, he replied, "I kept telling myself that I am the leader. I am in control. As long as I do not give it to them, they can not take it."

The confidence of control is the key to being an effective parent when it comes to influencing responsible behavior of your children with video games. But, be warned, one must be conscious of the fact that control will not be maintained without great effort, sometimes of the sacrificial variety. But that is the cost of being the quarterback. When you win, you get too much credit. When you lose, you get too much blame.

2. *You Must Become More Like a Terminal 12-year-old*

I get more frowns when I share this rule with parents than any of the other rules. As parents, we spend so much time and energy running away from our childhood. But if you are going to be a successful video game parent, you have to become more like a terminal 12-year-old. You have to have a demeanor that has the capacity to embrace the new and novel and enjoy the sheer pleasure that they offer. George Bernard Shaw said, *"We don't stop playing because we grow old; we grow old because we stop playing."*

Remember the days when you could be entertained with a simple toy and a situation constructed from make believe? Remember when you would dare to dream about things and not be shackled by fear of failure? You would just try it. Remember all those things that brought you joy that you do not do any more? Like getting into your car and going for a drive just to listen to your favorite music. How about spontaneously going out dancing and having a great time with friends? Remember the times when you could hardly catch your breath because you were laughing at yourself acting silly?

I am not saying that you should not be responsible and I am not saying that you should not exhibit mature behavior. I am saying that you can have both, and in the process, you will become closer to your children. In the end, it is that level of proximity that will allow you to have access in order to influence their lives. Don't forget what it is like to be a kid.

As Ben Carson said in his book, *The Big Picture*, "Children today come programmed with the same basic emotions children have always had. Because there are no new feelings, not even any updated versions of old emotions, we can better parent our children simply by thinking back to our childhood—remembering what we thought was fair and unfair, what we worried about, what hurt or embarrassed us, even what we thought we might be able to get away with. Remembering helps us empathize. It can help us be more patient. It may even help identify a warning flag that will help us spot potential trouble in time to head it off.

3. *Know Your Child First*

This rule is most often taken for granted. Every parent wants to brush by this one because they feel this is the one they have down pat. Parents frequently say, "I know my child. I brought this child into the world. I breast fed this child. I know my child!" Then you come home one day and your child is on the phone using words that would make a sailor cringe. Or you witness them hiding the newspaper from an elderly neighbor because they don't like her.

Getting to know your child does not happen by osmosis. It is not a passive process, and, if you do not know how to activate the process, seek help. Counseling can go a long way in helping to get things started. Knowing what makes your child tick can go a long way in helping you decide what video game titles your child should or shouldn't play.

Also, remember that one size does not fit all. If you have multiple children, your video game choice for one child is not necessarily the choice for another. If the children are close in age, your decision on a video game title should default to the child at greater risk. Notice that I did not use age as a deciding factor. In addition to knowing your child, you have to get to know their friends and their friends' home situations. Once your child leaves your house, they are subject to the environments of the homes they visit and other parents may not share your parenting standards.

4. Be Willing to Go Back to School

No parent falls out of the womb being a great video game chaperone. Therefore, you have to be willing to go to school and learn what you need to know. Many parents feel that video game content is the only parameter that needs to be known. I caution you to please remember that the devil is in the details and there are plenty of details associated with video games. I am not saying that you have to enroll in a video game development course at the local technical college, but I am suggesting that you try out online demos, and research the game on the web. Look at the packaging and get clues about the content. Visit the manufacturer's Website for additional information on the game before purchasing. There is a lot of ground that needs to be covered and you have to be willing to make this a priority.

5. Look at the Ratings With a Jaundiced Eye

Remember the ESRB ratings are a place to start, not a place to end. There are several ratings options available. Those options should be used in concert, not necessarily given exclusive dominion over the development of your video game policy for your child.

6. Time and Place Make a Difference

Make no mistake; too much of anything is always bad. And just like parents have always told us, there is a time and place for everything.

7. Let the Children Help Make the Rules

When setting the video game policy for your family, your children should be involved in the process. In fact, give them the first crack at developing it and putting it in writing. Of course, most of the time their first pass will be much too lenient. But they may surprise you! It makes no difference how appropriate their first draft is, you must shape the final document. And when it is all said and done, they would have been part of the process. Remember, when you muffle a voice, you ignite frustration and conflict.

8. Consequences Are a Fact of Life

I believe that at every opportunity, your child should be made aware of the rules of the game called life. For every action there is a consequence that must be anticipated and dealt with. Frequently, parents establish and maintain an almost make believe world for their children that does not obey the laws of the real world. We do our children a great disservice when this happens. Our attempts to shelter and protect, instead hinders the child's ability to succeed in life.

Once again, I refer to Ben Carson and his book, *The Big Picture*. He and his wife instituted a chip system to help their boys deal with issues of personal responsibility. I used the core of this system to fashion my own for video game parents. My suggestion is that children get chips (poker chips will do) for completing all of their responsibilities that are done in a timely fashion. The responsibilities are ones they help to define. The list of expectations is placed in strategic places around the house for all to see. When the dishes are done properly and on time, the child gets 20 poker chips. When a chore is late, but it gets done, the child only receives 10 chips. When you miss doing a chore and someone else has to complete it for you, you lose the 20 chips and you owe the house an additional 10.

This category of misbehavior is quite punitive and you can dig a hole very quickly. The amount of time that you have for playing video games is dependent upon what you have in your account. If you are completing all your responsibilities in a timely fashion, the more chips that you are able to earn. The chips are used to buy video game playtime, but they can be used for other desirable privileges as well. The catch is that you can only earn a maximum amount of privilege time. The total time in a week cannot exceed half the amount of time that you spend in school.

On the other hand, if you do not complete your responsibilities in a timely fashion, you have to suffer the consequences of your actions. You do not have enough in your account to allow you to play. If you want that situation to change, then get with the program. This system can be very effective in promoting responsible behavior. But remember to keep a lookout for the "chore chip" black market trade. Kids can get very creative. Of course, the system that you devise may be different, but the core of the exercise is that children must face the consequences of their actions when it relates to video game play.

9. The Family that Plays Together Stays Together

Today, parents and children must aggressively seek proximity with each other because of the shearing forces that the family unit encounters. Since video game play can command a large component of your child's time, plan family time around in-house or outside the home video game activities. Use video games as an asset to make contact with your child. It puts you in a position to really get to know them. It can help construct an early warning system about the development of important issues both in the present and in the future.

Parents should take this a step further and go to the video game store with their children and be involved in the purchase of titles. The kids usually go to the same place to buy their games. Get to know the manager. They can be the source of a wealth of information to get you up to speed and keep you abreast of the latest titles and technology. In addition, the manager and staff can give you hints on your child, their purchasing habits, and behavior when you are not with them.

10. *Parents Must Become a Band Of Brothers*

Parents must get rid of a bunker mentality and realize that to become a successful video game parent, it takes a village. In the past, a cadre of individuals, not always related, helped to raise most children. In today's society, this has changed. But with a little prioritized effort, this parenting asset can establish a circle of comrades that can help monitor your child's video game play, patterns and behavior.

The Internet makes this collaboration easier to achieve. But you have to be willing to organize. This is what the children do. They have organized their own local "World of Warcraft" guilds and will cart their computers from house to house to play. You have to have the same spirit of cohesiveness and collaborative execution. Parental teamwork can be the first and last line of defense when it comes to establishing a safety net for your child.

In this chapter, I have been very candid with my views on parents' responsibility in helping to control the video game play of their children. I want you to know that I realize being a successful parent in the video game age is not easy. But if we are to address the concerns about the welfare of our children, their education, and our country's future, the launching pad for a revolution of empowerment must begin with children that have a great awareness of the need for balance. Our mantra should be, "Every great nation is built on the shoulders of men and women who are good well-rounded citizens, and as a parent, I am committed to making sure that my child is one of them."

CHAPTER FOURTEEN

ⅤIDEO GAMES IN THE
21ST CENTURY CLASSROOM

A Visit To The Video Game Store

In June 2007, I was driving around in my car listening to music and just chillin', when I decided to stop at my favorite video game store. When I take a break from the never-ending chaos that clutters my life, I love going into the store to marvel at the gadgetry, the new titles, and to just chew the fat with the other gamers that come in. In my own way, I am checking the pulse of the 'state of the union' of video gaming.

This particular day was very unusual; there were only four people in the store. And interestingly, they all had a substantial amount in common. First, they were males between the ages of 19 and 23. They were all products of the public school system. They all loved playing video games. And finally, they had all experienced dropping out of school at some level.

The oldest of the bunch had reached his sophomore year in college before he dropped out, got a job, and never went back. He was the store manager. A second young man was the assistant manager. He dropped out of high school during his senior year. Another one was the manager of a store down the street and he was there hanging out on his break. He started his first year in college, then went home for a weekend visit and just never returned. The youngest dropped out of high school after his sophomore year. Additionally, these men had another shocking unexpected commonality—They all had IQ's over 130. What had gone wrong? These were pretty cool kids who exuded intelligence. Why were they not able to traverse our educational system? While I was there with them listening to their stories, I could not help but think back to a footnote in history.

In a State of The Union speech given before a joint session of Congress on January 31, 1990, George W. Bush gave the Senators and Congressmen the following vision and challenge:

"Education is the one investment that means more for our future because it means the most for our children. Real improvement in our schools is not simply a matter of spending more: Its a matter of asking more—expecting more—of our schools, our teachers, of our kids, of our parents, and ourselves. And that's why tonight I am announcing America's education goal; goals developed with enormous cooperation from the Nation's Governors. By the year 2000, every child must start school ready to learn. The United States must increase the high school graduation rate to no less than 90 percent. And we are going to make sure our schools' diplomas mean something. In critical subjects—at the 4th, 8th, and 12th grades—we must assess our students' performance. By the year 2000, U.S. students must be first in the world in math and science achievement."

I have a vivid memory of this portion of the speech because I thought that this could be one of the greatest leadership moments in American history. I equated it to the 1962 speech by John Kennedy when he told the country that by the end of the decade man would walk on the moon and it would be an American that would be the first to do it. President Kennedy's speech served to galvanize the nation with a singularity of purpose. And we not only achieved our goal, but also achieved it one year ahead of schedule. I felt in that portion of his speech in 1990, George H.W. Bush showed the same leadership initiative.

But yet in 2007, here I stood in a video game store with four brilliant individuals that had not maximized their potential. I was angry because I felt that a precious national resource had been squandered at a time when we needed all the help that we could get. Through the fog of the simmering anger, I tried to focus my frustration on a tangible target. Should I be angry with the young men for not realizing the blessing of intellect given to them? Should I be angry with the parents for not being proper chaperones to assure that their children stayed on task? As my mind cycled through the options for a target package, I stopped at the system. The system that George H.W. Bush had challenged to elevate; the national educational standard of excellence had in fact failed us all.

A Noble Gesture Who's Effort Fell Short

As I walked out of that video game store, I could not help but want to examine more closely what had gone wrong with something that was so right. The year 2000 had come and gone and I had just witnessed the unthinkable. Some of the best and brightest of our youth had been unable to maximize their intellectual potential. Things had in some ways become much worse since President Bush tried to do the "right thing." I became committed to acquiring the details about this travesty and the facts that I discovered would not prove to be pretty.

After my review, I found that the graduation rate in 2000 nationally had dropped to 69 percent, according to the Manhattan Institute for Policy Research—a long way from the 90 percent goal envisioned just a decade earlier. When compared to other countries, U.S. students that year ranked 22nd among 27 industrialized countries in math skills. In 2003, a similar study ranked U.S. students 24th of 29 countries.

The top ranked 15-year-old students (top 10 percent) in the United States ranked 21st out of 29 countries in math achievement in 2003, finishing behind the likes of Australia, Canada and France.

There are other facts that provide a sobering picture of the bleak landscape of the state of education in this country. According to the United States' Census Bureau, 367,000 students dropped out of high school in 2002. The true tragedy does not stop with social stigmatization because in addition, only 32.3 percent of high school dropouts ended up becoming employed.

The cost to the individual and to society when students drop out of school is staggering. A male high school graduate who works until age 65 will earn, on average, nearly $333,000 more than a dropout. Additionally, a worker with some college will earn $538,000 more. Finally, a male with a college degree will earn almost a million dollars, $945,670 more than a high school dropout.

The cost is not only to the individual. High school dropouts are a source of tremendous financial repercussions on society as a whole. According to research by Cecilia E. Rouse, a professor of economics and public affairs at Princeton University, high school dropouts contribute $60,000 less in federal and state income taxes over the course of a lifetime than individuals who receive their diploma. Thus, Rouse calculated that America loses more than $50 billion annually in federal and state income taxes from the 23 million high school dropouts aged 18 to 67, an amount nearly enough to cover the discretionary expenditures for the U.S. Department of Education in FY 2005 ($56.58 billion). Not only would tax revenue benefit from increasing the number of students who complete high school, but the burdens to the health care, public assistance, and criminal justice systems would receive relief as well. A one percent increase in high school graduation rates is projected to save approximately $1.4 billion in incarceration costs.

The problem with our education system does not stop with high school graduation rates. Even if a student successfully graduates from high school, a large percentage of students get their high school diplomas and are not prepared for college. According to data from the National Center for Education Statistics (NCES), approximately 28 percent of entering college freshmen had to take remedial courses in reading, writing or math in fall 2000. Nearly two in five college students say there were deficiencies in the education they received in high school.

The skills and work habits expected of them in college and the workforce were not adequately established. Over time, the costs of remedial courses eat away at student budgets and force many students to drop out or suspend their schoolwork so they can earn extra money or face deeper debt.

My review of the current educational state of the union was complicated by the fact that all data that suggests progress is not necessarily accurate. It is true that more students are enrolling in college today than a decade ago, but we must not be lulled to sleep by the use of college enrollment figures as a metric.

There is a perception that the majority of students who enter college actually graduate. This is a myth that only serves to lead us into a false sense of security. The fact is that for every 100 students who enter ninth grade, only about 69 graduate from high school, and just 38 of that original 100 go on to college. Finally, of the original number of students that start the ninth grade, only 18 of them wind up getting an Associate's or Bachelor's degree. These numbers are just not good enough and we have to do better.

The knowledge of these facts should cause all of us to scream for immediate reform. But most of us respond with a knee jerk band-aid reaction, just spend more and everything will be all right. This is yet another myth. Spending more money on education will not solve the problems. According to a study performed by The Manhattan Institute For Policy Research, "simply spending more money on education is not an acceptable solution to the dropout problem."

Finally, there is a "darker side" hidden behind the data just presented. If you look deeper, you see the true "tale of the tape" signaling that diversity, one of our strengths as a nation, is in a death grip of a "failure to thrive syndrome." White/European students will have about a 75 percent high school graduation rate, while African-American and Hispanic students have only about a 55 to 60 percent chance of graduating. And in many cities, it is much less than this.

Some would say that this is a sign of progress compared to the days of institutionalized discrimination and Jim Crow-facilitated exclusion. I would be the first to say that progress has in fact been made. But, all of this must be taken into proper context. The fact is, the high school graduation rate for Blacks and Hispanics is anemic. There needs to be a special effort to bring these statistics up to a higher completion rate. Our nation does not have the luxury of failing to tap into all its resources from all segments of our society.

A System Whose Time Has Come And Gone

Everyone wants to avoid the discussions about the 950 lb. gorilla in the room. It is the system and not the students that need the most attention. Microsoft founder Bill summed it up succinctly when he said:

America's high schools are obsolete. By obsolete, I don't just mean that our high schools are broken, flawed, and under-funded—though a case could be made for every one of those points. By obsolete, I mean that our high schools—even when they're working exactly as designed—cannot teach our kids what they need to know today…This isn't an accident or a flaw in the system; it is the system.

—Bill Gates, 2005

I think that Mr. Gates got it right. It is a fact that our current educational system is based on the needs of an agrarian economy in the 17th century and was never designed to function in the 21st century environment. Subsequently, the students of today are not prepared to compete in today's global economy.

Even our current school calendar is still influenced by a way of life that has passed by long ago. School starts in late summer/early fall. Historically, this coincided with the conclusion of crop and livestock tending season. The Thanksgiving break parallels crop harvest time. Christmas break is associated with a time reserved for canning, splitting wood, slaughtering, and storing meat products. Spring break was initially meant to sow seeds to plant new crops; not go to Daytona. And finally, the cycle completes itself with the summer break, which at one time was dedicated to tending the fields and raising the livestock.

With the advent of the industrial revolution, the same educational system was asked to turn out a small number of elite individuals; often the sons and daughters of the wealthy, who were groomed to become world class leaders. The rest were given a core curriculum that readied these students to become factory and manual labor workers. Today this system is still in place, but we no longer need to have farm or factory workers as the backbone of our national labor force. Quite frankly, the trend could be seen coming many years ago. At the turn of the 20th century, about 38 percent of the labor force worked on farms and by the end of the century, that figure was less than three percent. Likewise, the percentage of people who worked in industries such as mining, manufacturing and construction, decreased from 31 percent to 19 percent of the workforce. Service industries were the growth sector during the 20th century, jumping from 31 percent of all workers in 1900 to 78 percent in 1999 and this is not going to change in the near future.

If you take all of this into account, our country's educational system is at least *two economic models old and lagging badly behind the power curve.* For over 200 years, we were able to peacefully coexist with our current model. But after World War II, the body of mankind's knowledge began to expand at an exponential rate. With the advent of the race for space and the Cold War, there was an explosive expansion of knowledge in science and engineering. This is when the internal flaws of our system began to slowly become exposed. Somewhere between the 1970's and 1980's it began to simply fail. At first, career selection became skewed and now with the increasing dropout rates, the students are fleeing the system in record numbers.

Teaching to the Test Will Not Save Us

One aspect of President Bush's 1990 proclamations for education reform has been aggressively pursued. It is the introduction of proficiency tests onto the American educational landscape.

I strongly support testing and its ability to provide performance metrics, but I object to them being thrust upon the public without the provision of supportive assets necessary to make this action ultimately successful. As it stands, their emphasis appears to be just a politically expedient academic exercise. Unfortunately, they have become the poster child of current education reform efforts as leaders try to establish baseline levels of competency among our K-12 students.

The controversy surrounding proficiency testing is that all aspects of the system are heavily weighted toward test outcomes as if it is some magic bullet. School levies hang in the balance based on test scores. Teacher salaries, bonuses and even their right to teach are decided by the test results.

Cities that cannot raise their scores are being taken over by government. And when that happens, leadership is cutting the education process to the bare bones and "teaching to the test;" often at the expense of foreign language instruction, music and arts programs, as well as sports and fitness programs. This cannot be the educational renaissance that we want or need. Is our system of education to be relegated to a world of minimum compulsories that do not establish empowerment, but achieve a check in a completion box on some form? Are we destined to see a day when all students who achieve a diploma or degree pass their standardized tests but there are only a few that make it? And are those who make it able to transform facts inside their heads into real world functionality?

In the meantime, students are dropping out of school in record numbers. Some major cities such as Cleveland, Ohio and Chicago, Illinois, are currently experiencing dropout rates approaching 50 percent. A Time magazine article called "Drop Out Nation" gave some startling data. Not only are an average of 30 percent of students dropping out before finishing high school, but also 80 percent are passing when they do. Furthermore, in exit interviews, 100 percent site boredom as being a major factor for leaving.

The World of the Screens and Video Games: Forging a New System for the 21st Century

In spite of the sad state of affairs that our educational system finds itself in, we should not give up hope that this situation cannot be turned around. The brains of today's generation of students are laying dormant, waiting for an adjustment to the current system that will help unleash their full intellectual capacity. This opinion runs counter to many who feel this generation is flawed, spoiled and devoid of a good work ethic. Many say that they perpetually reside in a state of colossal distraction.

Conspiracy theorists would suggest that the entire generation carries a previously suppressed attention deficit disorder gene in their DNA. My response as a physician would be to ask a question. Could it be that the popularity of this diagnosis is based on criteria that are too liberal or flawed? Could it be that the symptoms of failure to focus—a short attention span and hyperactivity—the sign of an extremely advanced and capable brain crying out for more stimulation from the system?

Let's go a little deeper. What is the root cause of this problem? First, other "teachers" now tug on our children's learning time. And these teachers are outside of the traditional classroom environment. These new "teachers" dwell in what is called the world of the "screens." They first made their debut with the introduction of radio. I can hear those of you out there saying, "Butch, you have totally lost it. Everyone knows that a radio never had a screen." Before you call psychiatric services, think back to any image that you may have seen of a family sitting in a room listening to a radio. They are invariably looking at the radio as if they were looking at a picture.

It is true that there was no screen to look at, but I remember looking at the radio with my grandmother as we listened to a baseball game. There was no image presented, but my mind created the image that the technology could not. The movies presented the first screen that had widespread influence. Next, television began to infringe more and more on students' time. With the advent of the computer and the Internet, there has been an expansion of the effect from the world of the screens.

All of these new media carve into the time previously reserved for reading and other intellectual endeavors. As if things were not bad enough, the presence of screens in every aspect of daily life has increased with the introduction of sophisticated audio and video mobile devices. The students of today have these items at their disposal as a norm, not an exception. Is it no wonder that they seem distracted? *The only place that they do not have them in their lives is in school.* The challenge is to harness the world of the screens to serve as competent teacher assistants for this generation of students.

An important measure that must be considered if we are to put this concept into proper perspective is called "screen time." Screen time is the time spent during the course of a week in front of devices with a screen of some sort. To understand the magnitude of this untapped resource, it must be compared to the amount of instruction time an average student is exposed to in a traditional school environment.

In reshaping our current educational landscape we should first make simple adjustments. These include finding ways to extend the school day past the afternoon bell, and use some of the time that is spent in the world of the screens for education. There is no need to fight bloody battles over curriculum content. Let's concentrate on how to gain more opportunities for learning.

This effort should center on what I call the procurement of "screen hang time" for learning. One of the many physical attributes of Michael Jordan that made him a great basketball player was his ability to seemingly hang in mid-air while he executed a scoring opportunity. Michael had an uncanny ability to leap into the air. He would be still going up while his opponents were going down. This gave him a tremendous advantage because he had more time to decide what move he would make. Yes, it is true that he possessed tremendous athletic ability, but his basketball skills were superior because he also had a high basketball IQ. This was made possible because he was able to hang in the air and study an opponent longer before he made a decision on what to do.

School Time Vs. Screen Hang Time

I would now like to take you on a time management journey to compare the time spent for educational activities in the school, and the potential educational opportunities in the world of the screens. If you consider that the average school day begins at 8:15 am and is over at 3:15 pm, children are under the school's roof for seven hours. Remove lunch period, time to switch classes and time used for any physical education, music or art etc., and you only have the student in a classroom environment for about 5.5 to 6 hours per day, or at best, 27.5 hours per week.

In this era of the screens, television time has not decreased and students spend about 20 hours a week in front of this screen. The average adolescent student spends up to 13 hours playing video games. The Internet usage varies greatly and can average 5-10 hours or greater per week. Cell phone usage, including text messaging, can be a tough number to run down but an average of 5.4 hours per week has been sited. IPods and similar appliances are being increasingly used and data is very sketchy, but let us assume that it is just as prevalent as cell phone use.

When tabulated, the average time spent in school with educational activities is 27.5 hours. This is then compared with an average of 54 hours spent in the world of the screens. If we could claim a small percentage of "screen hang time" for education, we could make a great first step toward improving the effectiveness of the system. As with Michael Jordan, a small increase in hang time can be the difference between greatness and mediocrity.

How Video Games Can Fuel A Revolution In Education

It is not a stretch to believe that video games could have benefits for our educational system. In an earlier chapter, I give rather extensive evidence of the educational benefits of video games. In view of this overwhelming evidence, the most avid video game haters are starting to consider that there might be a small amount of good that can come from video games. But old habits are difficult to break.

These determined individuals take the fall back position that video games only have manual skill and dexterity development assets. This could not be further from the truth. Video games have the ability to enhance cognitive transfer as well. Just consider these findings. Students remember only 10 percent of what they read; 20 percent of what they hear; 30 percent, if they see visuals related to what they are hearing; 50 percent, if they watch someone do something while explaining it. But they retain almost 90 percent, if they do it themselves, even if only as a simulation.

There is ample evidence that points to the mainstream being more than just curious about video games and their learning assets. Many respected individuals and organizations have accepted their potential to address our educational dilemma. The Federation of American Scientists, the Entertainment Software Association, and the National Science Foundation convened a National Summit on Educational Games, on October 25, 2005 in Washington, D.C.

The Summit brought together nearly 100 experts to discuss ways to accelerate the development, commercialization and deployment of a new generation of games for learning.

Some of their findings are as follows:

- The video game industry has technology, tools tradecraft and talent that, with support, can be transferred and applied to the development of games for learning.
- Educational institutions need to transform organizational systems and instructional practices to take greater advantage of new technology, including educational games.

- Educational materials publishers, educational software producers, and game companies should explore the economics of developing and marketing browser-based and "downloadable" educational games.

- With video game consoles in more than 45 million homes, game companies or educational materials and educational software producers should explore developing educational games and simulations for home use (a call for screen hang time)

- When individuals play modern video and computer games, they experience environments in which they often must master the kinds of higher-order thinking and decision-making skills employers seek today. In addition, educational games that incorporate simulations provide a way to bridge the gap between abstract concepts or theoretical knowledge and practical skills, an important way to translate what is learned in training to application in the workplace.

Doug Lowenstein, President of the Entertainment Software Association and a participant in this symposium, said:

"Everywhere we turn, we hear more about visionary people recognizing how games can help train first responders, how they can help prepare surgeons (a reference to my research), how they can help kids manage pain, how they can help prepare air traffic controllers and software engineers. Does it make any sense that we can acknowledge all of this, but we can't acknowledge that games can help kids learn about the American Revolution, or the Middle Ages, or that they can help kids learn about biology or physics, or they can help kids understand economics?"

Clearly there has been more than a credible call for a change in the course of our educational methodologies and policies. It is also painfully apparent that the system's performance cannot be tolerated much longer. Others and myself are not calling for the death of all that it offers, but surely we can agree that our education system is in need of an upgrade. The argument should not be focused on "what should be taught," it should focus on "how it should be taught." Video game-inspired, and assisted lesson plans should have a large role to play in this renaissance.

Advanced Learning Techniques Contained In Video Games

Probing

Unlike Checkers or Monopoly, the rules that construct the play in the video game world are often not neatly packaged. At first glance, some would view this as a negative feature. Video gamers are forced to rapidly identify the ultimate goal of the game, and formulate and execute techniques that allow them to succeed in the game. They learn by playing. Some would call this "trial and error" or "experiential" learning. To traditional educators this would seem to be a deadly flaw, rather than a great learning asset. This technique taught with video games is called *probing*.

As a surgeon and scientist, I am very familiar with probing because it is at the heart of all scientific investigation. Probing represents an expression of scientific method, a reproducible process that accurately defines the unknown. James Paul Gee described it best and Steven Johnson gave further clarification.

Probing is a four part process that consists of an initial probe (initial investigation), formation of a hypothesis, re-probe, and rethink. The initial *probing* of the physics of the game (what control does what and how the game is played) establishes what scientists would call a *control*. This becomes the standard with which all investigations are compared.

With the control established, the player has an idea of which visual prompts, reoccurring events, control actions and sensitivity relates to being successful in playing the game. This allows the player to formulate a *hypothesis* or hunch on how the game should be successfully played. Next, you must re-probe or play the game again using rules established from your first experience. This tests your hypothesis. In essence, the player is verifying whether or not their hunches about playing the game are correct.

If the hunch is correct, the player places this data in their mental game rulebook. If their hypothesis is incorrect, the player *rethinks* the initial intuition by trying other alternative actions or tactics. The process is then repeated over and over again until the formula for successfully playing the game is established and mastered.

You don't have to be a rocket scientist to consider the advantages this could be to students or employees alike. When probing is mastered, an individual becomes very efficient at sifting through the clutter of insignificant data and establishing and maintaining focus on data that is relevant to the task at hand. They also are very comfortable with a blank sheet of paper and the unknown. They will default to using scientific methods to establish parameters where there are none known. Possessing this trait is the birthplace of innovation.

A new generation of students and employees will emerge possessing not just a head full of facts, but more resourcefulness, productivity and adaptability. Finally, because they are intimately aware of scientific methodology, considering a career in science, technology, engineering, medicine and mathematics will soon be the rule, not the exception.

Telescoping

Another cerebral attribute of video games that can become a staple item in upgrading our educational system is *telescoping*. This is a video game collateral learning asset also identified by Steven Johnson. He describes telescoping as the skill of managing the workflow required to accomplish several objectives simultaneously to successfully achieve a focused goal. He uses the example of how a telescope has many sections that collapse upon each other, the proper deployment of each one being important for it to serve its function. With video gamers there is always the game within the game that provides riddles to ultimate success. In order to win, these challenges must be successfully addressed.

Johnson is quick to point out that telescoping is not the same as multitasking. Many people are harboring a hoax when they extol the virtues of being able to multitask. They behave as if it is a testimony to, and a symbol of, intellectual ascension. Far from this premise, I believe that multitasking is a cousin of intellectual chaos. It only distinguishes one's ability to handle a disjointed stream of unrelated tasks. It is not a sign of intellectual maturity and superiority, but rather a symbol of an individual's entrapment in a web of sensory noise and overload.

Whenever I get an applicant seeking to become one of my research assistants, I am very detailed in letting them know the demands of the job. I warn that they will have long hours and that they will have many projects they successfully have to accomplish. The one response that I absolutely hate to hear is, "Don't worry, I am good at multitasking." As far as I am concerned, this response is good for a one-way ticket out the door. Just because you can handle many tasks at one time, does not mean that you will be a successful project manager.

On the other hand, a student who is good at telescoping is a creature committed to order. Johnson suggests that a person who masters telescoping is excellent at constructing a proper hierarchy of tasks and moving through the tasks in the correct sequence to accomplish an objective. They are adept at doing this not just once but consistently. These individuals are also able to focus on immediate challenges and still not lose sight of the ultimate objective. In the practice of surgery, telescoping is essential to a surgeon being an angel of healing and not a well-compensated assassin. The successful completion of an operation proceeds through a series of challenges presented by a patient's anatomy and their disease. All of the obstacles must be successfully overcome if the patient is going to survive.

Whenever I perform a surgical procedure, I approach each surgery with a similar posture. No matter what obstacle I face, I always focus and address the immediate needs at hand, all while keeping the sequence of the operation in mind and the ultimate goals of the procedure in play at all times.

As a surgeon, I must acknowledge that there are some colleagues that have all the necessary facts in their heads to be a great surgeon but they cannot perform procedures with low complication or mortality rates. I call them podium surgeons. They can talk a good game. They know all the jargon and they can tell you what to do. But they are unable to execute within the narrow margins of error that are demanded. Many factors go into the making of a surgeon, and skill level is one of them. But skill is not the sole determining factor of a successful operation or a good surgeon. Good decision-making is a trait that is common to all master surgeons. Lack of good decision-making is frequently a common trait of all podium surgeons.

It is a surgeon's ability to know when and where to cut and not just how to cut that determines if an individual is one of the greatest surgeons of all times or a legend in their own mind.

I would rather have a surgeon who is a master of probing and telescoping than one who scored in the 93rd percentile on a qualifying exam but has inefficient decision-making skills. All of this has real world relevance. Over 100,000 patients die each year from medical errors and 57 percent of these deaths are from surgical errors. The utilization of video games as an adjunct to medical education will more efficiently advance the surgeon's ability to probe and telescope. This is not a pipe dream to be dismissed, but a hypothesis that demands exploration.

Engaged Consequentiality

I recently had the privilege of being invited to a function in Chicago hosted by the MacArthur Foundation. This historic philanthropic leader has launched a $50 million initiative to investigate video games and their impact on society, and more importantly, how they can be harnessed for purposes other than entertainment. One of the panelists was Dr. Shasha

Barab from Indiana University. I was really drawn to this person because of his gritty authenticity and I thought that he was really cool, down to Earth and touchable. He is a practicing gamer and an intellectual that has the ability to bridge theory with reality.

During his talk, he introduced a new learning concept called *engaged consequentiality*. This is a video game-based learning technique featuring an engaging storyline (narrative), interactive rule sets, ever-present reward structure, and rich 2D or 3D virtual environments. This innovative approach holds the learner's attention by embedding the lessons to be learned into real-world context. Another feature is that the student is suspended in a situational immersion in which they are in control of their actions and their actions have consequences. Hence the name *engaged consequentiality*.

Wow, talk about a Kodak moment; I got the angle of this approach right away. It is a lesson plan that has at its core an engine that is based on simulation of real life situations. If you are going to excel, *you have to practice before you play*. This is a training approach that NASA and the aerospace industry have used to establish a legacy of excellence. Engaged consequentiality can find traction in many educational arenas including the modern day practice of surgery.

Barab's approach challenges the age-old standard in education that knowledge is a thing to be acquired and it is a cognitive act that takes place in the confines of isolated minds. I agree with Barab that knowledge is an activity that is embodied; it is a by-product of individual-environmental interaction that involves the totality of the human experience.

If this theory is to be accepted, one must accept the premise that true education and functional empowerment can best be established when the lesson plan objectives have dynamic, contextual, real world relevance. Facts are only important if they have relevance. This is not to say that facts are not important. They just do not have supreme importance. Historically, we have assumed that domain formalizations will be automatically relevant to real-life situations, but there is no data to verify this. The documentation of a student's possession of facts only provides comfort to policy makers, school administration officials, teachers and some parents. But, the truth is that our schools are not creating critical thinkers who function effectively in the real world. As a result, we are losing students from the educational process at an alarming rate.

Engaged consequentiality could recruit individuals to the educational process because students can learn while having fun. Once engaged students will experience more transfer of knowledge. The key to a more effective future for education in this country depends on adjusting the delivery of current curriculums. Facts should be presented within an enriched knowledge narrative where they are tools for understanding and behaving in real-life situations, not academic trophies to be memorized and worshiped.

In the future, curricula that use this approach will take the student on a journey in which the learner's decision-making has consequences in advancing a lesson story line. Choice A will advance a student down a different storyline than choice B, just as they do in video games. As the journey unfolds, new information is unveiled and learned. The learner aggressively seeks the possession of facts because it facilitates the successful progression of the narrative.

Barab's initial studies have identified that this way of teaching is more effective than traditional techniques. He is committed to identifying customized scaffolding endoskeletons and attaching subject matter facts. These will serve as the core for engaged consequentiality lesson plans. I too am committed to conducting such investigations, and I look forward to the day when this learning method will become the norm.

As I come back to video games—my first love, I am very excited by the prospect of this approach being helpful in training surgeons. The monumental amount of facts involved in making surgical treatment decisions could be neatly compartmentalized according to the situation that a surgeon faces. Subsequently, these facts are leveraged into a decision-making flow based on real world clinical situations. They are released from the confines of bound pages, and come alive to help heal and save lives. Remember, the surgeon who possesses the most memorized facts is not necessarily the one that you want to perform your operation.

The Power of Video Games in the Classroom: A Real World Example

It is one thing to discuss what video games can offer to students and teachers in the classroom setting; it is another thing to actually implement and document this hypothesis with metrics that show a distinct advantage to this type of learning over the gold standard. One such example is the project done by social studies teacher, David McDivitt, at Oak Hill High School in Converse, Indiana.

Converse is a small town in Northeast Indiana with a population of just over 1,200. In retrospect, the small size of the school system was an advantage. Another factor was that at the initiation of his project there were no rules or regulations for, or against video games to assist in the classroom. Mr. McDivitt was also a well-respected member of the community. As the high school football coach, he had earned a reputation as being willing to do anything to help "his kids." There came a time when Mr. McDivitt became very concerned about the effectiveness of his teaching. He saw his classroom invaded by more and more electronic gadgets. "The teenagers walking into my classroom have iPods, cell phones (with movies on them), and twitching fingers from constant IMing, and video games. I had to do something." These "techno termites" were eating away at Mr. McDivitt's students' focus and time on their studies. His idea was not to swim up stream against the current, but rather, just go with the flow. He decided to use video games as an adjunct to his lesson plan in history.

When he ran across an advertisement for a new educational video game called "Making History" by Fuzzy Lane software, he instantly knew that he had a test for his hypothesis that a video game could enhance achievement beyond grade level expectations. At the time, there was no blue print on how to do this. He started with a blank sheet of paper and a heart that was brimming with confidence that he was doing the right thing.

In his study, he selected a very focused time in history. The events in Europe circa 1938 that eventually led to the beginning of World War II. His hypothesis was that students using the video game-enhanced curriculum would learn at a superior level than those educated in the traditional fashion. Using a total of 110 students, he devised two control groups and three experimental groups. He had three classes totaling 65 students use the video game exclusively, and 45 students in two classes used the traditional textbook and lecture method of learning the same subject. The video game group never opened a textbook and did not have homework assignments. The traditionally-taught control groups had the usual textbooks, homework and reading assignments.

The only teaching technique that was shared by both groups was class discussion sessions about the material reviewed. Pre-testing and post-testing of both groups in the concepts of European leadership and causes for war, as well as European geography allowed measurement of the learning levels achieved by the two methods used. The pre-teaching and post-teaching test questions were identical for all groups.

The first thing Mr. McDivitt noticed was the excitement generated by bringing an electronic teaching method into the classroom, and the increased level of interest and participation. The interest in his "video game history class" even spilled out into the hallways and cafeteria of the school to impact others. He overheard discussions about different historical events and tactics used in playing the game. Students even came to his classroom after school wanting to have another opportunity to play!

During the classroom discussion sessions, Mr. McDivitt noticed a marked difference in the depth of discussions taking place in the video game-taught groups than the traditionally-taught control groups. Objectively, he discovered that the video game-instructed classes outperformed the traditionally-taught classes in all measured areas.

The students who participated in the video game-enhanced curriculum had superior test scores when compared to the traditional groups. The areas measured included knowledge of European geography (70 percent/45 percent), meaning of the Munich conference (90 percent/55 percent), reasons for the start of World War II (67 percent/35 percent), and similarities between Soviet Communism and Nazi Germany (82 percent/72 percent). The results all favored the video game-assisted course.

With this level of demonstrated success, Mr. McDivitt suggests that educators across the country begin to seriously consider investigating the feasibility of formally incorporating video games into lesson plans as a teaching tool. He argues that leadership should support the efforts of teachers who try to lead the way toward validating these system upgrades with good science.

Despite his enthusiasm, Mr. McDivitt does caution that video games should be an enhancement to, and not a replacement of, traditional methods. I salute the efforts of Mr. McDivitt and the many others like him who have yet to be recognized. He is a living example of what makes this country so special. Often our finest hour is forged from the depths of desperation and despair. This is a feat that has been chronicled many times over in this nation's history.

As we move on from this topic, I hope that proponents of this strategy will not become totally focused on the production of titles. Flooding the market with titles that all proclaim to be the magic bullet to end the ills of education in this country will not be the answer. Rather, we must be disciplined and use the approach utilized by Mr. McDivitt.

Our objective should be to surround the learner in an educational ecosystem that will result in students feeling empowered to perform to their potential. Because of Mr. McDivitt's efforts, my heart is filled with absolute optimism that in the future the scene at the video game store with my young friends will become a rare occurrence.

CHAPTER FIFTEEN
VIDEO GAMES AND EDUCATION
TEAM UP TO BEAT OBESITY

It was late on a hot summer night in Baton Rouge, Louisiana in August 2005. Debra Tilson was having difficulty sleeping as her air conditioner was fighting a losing battle to maintain a comfortable setting in the face of the oppressive humidity and oven-like temperatures. She turned on the television to see if it could work its usual magic and lull her to sleep. Work had followed her home this evening because she was unsettled about the future of her beloved Southern University.

She loved that institution and its students like family. Her allegiance began when she received her diploma after being a student there from 1992-1997. She was proud of that diploma and rightfully so. Her road to a degree had not been a traditional one. She was 31-years-old when she started.

After graduating with honors from high school, she married her high school sweetheart and immediately started a family. Instead of beginning her college education, she started a 14-year career as a stay at home mom. Make no mistake about it, she took her job seriously and loved taking care of her children. Because she worked so hard taking care of her family, she cherished her free time and spent it playing her favorite video games. She had always been a fan of technology and loved playing *Centipede*, *Ms. Pac Man* and *Burger Time*.

All of this came crashing to an end when her husband Emile suffered a serious back injury at work. There would be many changes in the Tilson household. Since her children were older, Debra felt this could be the chance to realize her dream of getting her college degree and help support the family. She and her husband prayed about it and after going through the application process, she enrolled at Southern in 1992.

In spite of all of the challenges in her life, she received her degree. After graduation she stayed on to work in the information technology department and was assigned to the library. Proud of her degree and her school, she carried with her an intense allegiance to Southern University. Southern had been there for her and had given her a chance. In spite of all the progress our nation has made in the last 200 years, there are still some large loopholes in the education and opportunity safety net for persons of color. Thank God that a Southern University still exists and remains loyal to its mission to be there for the Debra Tilsons of the world.

On this night, the question of the university's relevance in a 21st century America had become a serious debate from the state house to Washington, D.C. Did the country still require historically black institutions? Do these entities still serve a purpose that is truly needed today? In addition, she was troubled because corporations have politely suggested that they have job opportunities but they were finding it very difficult to fill those positions with African-Americans because of a lack of qualified candidates.

For Debra, this was a great disappointment and left her in disbelief. As far as she was concerned, there was a great disconnect between what corporations said was out there and what she saw everyday in the outstanding students on her campus. Even harder to swallow was the insinuation that minority students could probably be considered in the future if they were better prepared in college. It angered her to think of the prospect of giving credence to such an implication. While she was pondering all of this, her eyes were closed but she was wide awake. The whine of the air conditioner struggled unsuccessfully to cool her room and she could not get her mind off the fact that her beloved university was at a point where desperate measures had to be taken, immediately.

She then directed her attention to lighter thoughts. Video games had always played a recreational role in her life, and she thought it would be great if they could help with the plight of the students at Southern University. The chancellor had recently announced a challenge to everyone at the university to brain storm and come up with cutting-edge ideas that could make the university competitive for grant dollars by submitting ideas or innovations that were on or beyond the cutting-edge.

To her credit, she had been trying, but in spite of the efforts, she had nothing to show for it. Just that morning, her hopes had been dashed by the failure of her latest grant attempt. By the time she got home earlier in the evening, it seemed that it was a struggle to breathe; she had all but given up hope. Tired of replaying her nightmare over and over, with disgust, she slowly turned her back to the television to try once again to settle in for some much-needed sleep. When she was like this, she would leave the television on to help her doze and it began to work.

At that moment, she heard the TV announcer say that a feature was coming up about a surgeon who had done research documenting that video games could be used to improve the skill and accuracy of surgeons. This revelation got her attention and then she heard a booming voice and a big belly laugh. She quickly turned over, almost bumping her husband out of the bed. She was met by this big smile from this big guy who by her report seemed to light up the darkness of her bedroom. She hung on every word and at the end of the piece; her despair had been transformed into a bastion of hope.

The next morning she was determined to talk to this guy who was an African-American and had a funny name, Dr. Butch Rosser. Yes, I was the person that she had seen on television. Using the Internet, she put my name into the search engine and she found my location, website and phone number. This is scary!

Debra took a deep breath and called. Wouldn't you know it; I was out of the country. Debra made a mental note to call the next week. But, it was a call that was not made, because on August 29, 2005 her world would be turned upside down. On that day her beloved Louisiana was assaulted by one of the worst natural disasters in the history of the United States... Hurricane Katrina.

Needless to say, other priorities took precedence as everyone pulled together to support the relief effort. Then on January 24, 2006, she was looking for someone else's number and ran across mine. She called again and my administrative assistant made an appointment for her to call me the following week. When she called, to her surprise I answered the phone. She almost swallowed her tongue but she managed to say, "Hi, my name is Debra Tilson. I am nobody that would register on your radar screen and I don't know what to say to you." I gave out a big laugh and then gathered myself to finally say, "Girl, I'm from Mississippi and everybody is somebody to me. You can say what you want and I will listen."

After the telephone conference with Mrs. Tilson, I did my background research on Southern University. I did not have to do much because it is one of the most recognized historically Black institutions in the nation. In the past, it has been one of the few universities of its kind that offered advanced degrees for people of color, and it has been around since 1879. Its alumni have a reputation of being very capable and have a profile of excellence in national leadership for the country. In addition, their football team and band have a track record of exemplary and legendary performance. I had a special vantage point as to the accuracy of Southern's prowess, because I lived 11 miles from Mississippi Valley State University, one of its rivals in the Southwest Athletic Conference. This conference is the home of football powerhouses such as Grambling, Jackson State University and Southern University.

I could not help but embrace what she felt toward the institution. I wanted to be of help, but I knew that it would take a radical demonstration to attract funding. I firmly believed that with the right combination of guidance and collaborative assets, the University could help pave the way for a monumental advancement in the way children were taught. Southern had all the raw materials to make it happen. It had the right mission statement that focused on training the teachers of tomorrow. It had a strong college of education with visionary and capable leadership that was eager to look beyond the horizon and committed to bring the institution to the next level.

The institution had an underdog's attitude with a chip on its shoulder. The only thing that could remove that chip was the achievement of their goal of becoming recognized as one of the best institutions of higher learning in the world. I could smell a sense of controlled desperation. The same thing that a coach longs to smell in the locker room before his team takes the field for a big game that everybody expects them to lose. I will go to battle with these kinds of folks every time, win or lose.

A prime asset of the University is the fact that they have a laboratory school on its campus. The school provides course work for grades pre-k to high school. Current student enrollment at the laboratory school is 530 students. The Southern University laboratory school has played a pivotal role in the education of young African-American students for almost a century. Conceived in 1914 and officially recognized as a University based school in 1922, it has steadfastly been the bedrock for introducing advanced teaching methodology for students of color in Louisiana and beyond. There is a 97 percent to 100 percent graduation rate.

The laboratory school is intimately associated with the College of Education at Southern University. Its current chairperson, Dr. Janis People, has often commented that, "the Southern laboratory school serves a role similar to that of an academic teaching hospital seen in medical education. It is a place where the most cutting-edge knowledge transfer modalities are to be studied and validated." Its current headmaster, Dr. Derek Morgan is determined to maintain the core of its founding energies and to sustain a tradition of excellence and of perpetual innovation.

Dr. Johnny Tolliver, Vice Chairman for Academic Affairs, and a former Army artillery officer, is a recent addition to the Southern faculty, and has a long track record as an innovator. A meeting was arranged for leadership and faculty with the objective of identifying a research target that could achieve our ambition. All were very supportive in taking on an ambitious project that could be a paradigm shift in the way we teach our students. We identified a target that involved addressing three icons in today's society: education, videogames and obesity.

Obesity is a healthcare concern of global proportions. In 2005, the Centers for Disease Control and Prevention surveyed the United States population and 60.5 percent of people were overweight and 23.9 percent were obese. But the penetration of this killer in the adult population is not the true indicator of the threat posed to the population at large in the future. This will become an issue of increasing concern for years to come because of the alarming incidence of obesity in our children. Between 1999 and 2000, the number of overweight Americans was 15.5 percent among 12- to 19-year-olds, 15.3 percent among 6- to 11-year-olds, and 10.4 percent among 2- to 5-year olds. This is compared with 10.5 percent, 11.3 percent, and 7.2 percent, respectively, between 1988-1994.

This problem is no longer a problem limited to the United States. In 2002, the World Health Organization warned that obesity is a global issue affecting the entire world. The effects can be seen in India, Bangladesh, and rural fishing villages from the west coasts of South Africa and Nigeria. It is a significant problem in urban areas of China. In a study published in the August 2006 issue of the Australian Family Physician, 30.2 percent of Australian children under the age of 18 were overweight or obese, with 18.1 percent being overweight and 12.1 percent being obese. Childhood obesity rates have tripled in Australia since 1985.

These are shocking statistics. The effect of being overweight and obese on an individual's health is far-reaching. Obesity has been linked to many deadly diseases. These include diabetes, cardiovascular disease, renal failure, stroke, cancer, high blood pressure, sleep apnea and others. Childhood obesity is the incubator for these diseases that produce the most morbidity and mortality in our society. It also threatens our ability to continue our species because it is a leading cause of infertility. The Office of the Surgeon General reports that obesity is responsible for as many as

300,000 premature deaths each year. This is why obesity has been crowned public enemy number one on the healthcare most wanted list.

In spite of the billions spent each year in weight loss programs and products in this country, the literature shows there is only negligible permanent weight loss, no matter what diet program you try. Surgery has made great strides to help those who are morbidly obese and it is the only permanent weight loss treatment option. But this is an extreme procedure that should be used in only select circumstances. It is not a treatment mainstay that should be relied upon for the general population.

I speak on this issue from a unique vantage point as a victim of childhood and adult morbid obesity, a physician, a surgeon that performs the gastric bypass procedure, and a patient that was saved by the knife. But as I give this testimony today, it is because I had to risk my life to save my life by undergoing a life-saving laparoscopic gastric bypass procedure.

I was 460 pounds before the surgery and now, seven years later I weigh 290 pounds. There is a rebirth that has occurred in my life but I had to resort to extreme measures. Clearly the answer to this epidemic does not reside with an operation. It will only be found within the privy of prevention. And prevention must start early with the children through education. This is the path that must be taken if we are to put my knife out of business. A historical precedent for the possible success of this approach can be found in the campaign to institute universal compliance for seat belt use for driving safety. An important contributor to today's success was the public service awareness campaigns that targeted schools and children from kindergarten to university.

The next feature of our project would reside in the field of education. I have spent a significant amount of effort earlier in this book stating my position on the need to upgrade the system by introducing more effective methodologies into the classroom that can inspire, recruit and retain students' interest so they can show the full extent of their intellectual muscle. The final component is the use of video games to help achieve our educational goals. The platform that would serve to launch the Southern/Rosser collaborative effort is called the *Digital Curriculum Conversion Project*.

This project seeks to investigate the feasibility and effectiveness of the use of an over-the-counter 3D animated movie, a digital interactive video game "Body Mechanics," video game fitness titles and customized digital interactive curriculum enhancements put forth in a classroom lesson plan that fulfills grade level expectations (GLE). The program adheres to rigorous Louisiana state and national curriculum standards for K-6th grades in the STEM (Science, Technology, Engineering and Mathematics) curriculum categories.

The project seeks to utilize an AKA (Awareness, Knowledge and Action) strategy for success. The 3D Body Mechanics movie/game will make the children aware of the childhood obesity problem. It will help transfer strategic physiologic facts to K-6th graders using the power of a digital interactive medium. The transfer of knowledge will then be reinforced and tested by the video game-based interactive challenge program. Next, the students will be called to action by playing the activity-based video game, *Dance Dance Revolution*. This project will evaluate the student performance in GLE and the program's impact on weight loss and wellness. Here is some background on the critical components of this program.

Dance Dance Revolution

Dance Dance Revolution is one of the hottest and bestselling video games. It is revolutionizing how children get fit. It is being used as the latest weapon in the battle against the epidemic of childhood obesity. *Dance Dance Revolution* can be described as having an "exertion interface," compelling players to exercise while having fun playing a video game. This combination of "exercise" and "video game" play can be termed "exergaming," because it makes players want to get up and move. *Dance Dance Revolution* keeps children from becoming victims of inactivity. The game even lets you know how many calories you're burning while dancing.

Body Mechanics

The Body Mechanics 3D movie and interactive video game is designed to help parents and kids win the battle for better health by teaching them how their bodies work, and providing the tools to achieve an active and healthy lifestyle while engaging in a **fun** and **entertaining environment**. A 3D animated action adventure movie that integrates learning with the thrill of fast-paced animation will introduce children to complex body functions in the context of a captivating battle inside the body between good and evil.

The movie and the game put a "face" to disease processes that exist inside their bodies. Health issues are given authenticity by presenting them in an entertaining style and in a digital interactive format that children crave. Different skill levels allow players to be challenged at their individual pace.

The Process

First, a special curriculum committee reviewed the movie and game with great detail. This committee was made up of educators from the University and Laboratory school. Subject matter categories were identified in the game. These were coordinated with standardized curriculum unit parameters. After determining the proper unit designation of the material in the game, these were matched with curriculum requirement GLE. The GLE were correlated with the state and national curriculum guide resource for K-6th grades. We then identified the Body Mechanics product features that could be used without modifications.

Additional programs or products needed to fulfill curriculum requirements were accounted for, and customized or enhanced programs and products were conceptualized. Next, a curriculum developmental process, validation methodology, time line and preliminary budget were formulated.

The program was divided into multiple phases. Phase I is the initial introduction of the program into the culture of the school with an event similar to the Top Gun 4 Kids program previously described in this book. This will expose the students and the teachers to the format before it is introduced. Initial satisfaction and feedback data will be collected.

With the help of the Digital Curriculum Conversion committee, the designated curriculum items will be converted into the upgraded format and all identified customized elements will be perfected. This phase will last six months. Phase II will be a pilot program to establish contact with the teachers and students. This will be accomplished with an after school program led by a mixture of Laboratory School teachers and Southern University College of Education graduate students.

During the three-month trial, satisfaction queries from students, teachers, and assessment portfolios, will serve as the metrics for objective evaluation of the program. We will then create a professional development program for teachers selected to administer the program. This will be a two-week summer program to train the teachers by familiarizing them with instructional strategies and digital interactive media that will be used in the classroom. It will help establish competencies in using the technology needed to execute the curriculum and assess the teachers in simulated classroom situations. Phase IV will be the launch of the program in the regular school session. At the end of the school year, Phase V will involve data analysis, a final report, and a white paper.

Each step of the way, the curriculum committee will oversee the progression of the project. They will look at factors that demonstrate that the video game-based curriculum fulfills all designated curriculum requirements. They will oversee the credentialing of the teachers and monitor their performance. Also, all data will be presented and evaluated as the program progresses by the governing board for curriculum validation at the College of Education, and the governing board will pass final judgment on the adequacy of validation of the curriculum.

Formulization of this project was accomplished in less than four months and the journey was truly an exciting experience. This effort dispels the myth that nebulous concepts always take a long time to reach a substantive state. I found that motivated, large institutions could move with speed and efficiency when they have great personnel with big hearts and passion. The Internet was key to facilitating the intense collaboration of the group. But, it was entertaining to see the dynamics of the antics behind closed doors in our real world work group sessions. Nobody would believe the fun that was to be had. These highly trained and well-respected educators took on this project as if they were truly terminal 12-year-olds. I had the privilege to be their fearless leader and I was in my element combining fun with the attack of a highly complex problem. At the end of a planning period, a 47 page document was produced that provided details of a cutting edge, innovative, educational empowerment platform that not only addressed educational method deficiencies, but also contemporary issues surrounding health and the public welfare. The project has been submitted for funding and encouraging feedback has been forthcoming. I look forward to reporting the results of this program in the near future.

Just think… all of this occurred because of a bout of insomnia on a hot muggy August night in Baton Rouge, Louisiana. The actions of Debra Tilson, who thought she was no one special, showed that an ordinary person who stepped out on faith for the benefit of others could be the driving force behind something that could not only benefit today's students, but the health of a nation. It is a lesson that all of us should take away: great things are not solely accomplished by what resides within your cranial vault, but great things are accomplished because of what resides within your chest, the heart. When a person faces obstacles to obtaining a difficult goal, they cannot rationalize or intellectualize their way around them. They must be willing to show an unwavering commitment to the cause, and depend on that thing called passion to transform the impossible into reality.

Part Six

TAKING THE REVOLUTION BEYOND EDUCATION:

WHY WE CAN WIN

After the previous section, it would be natural to have a great deal of enthusiasm about the prospect of the collateral learning assets found in video games helping to better educate our children in K-16. But, it is the impact of these assets to influence our way of life beyond the classroom that is the lynchpin on which the future of this nation hinges. Evidence abounds about the ability of video games to enhance our healthcare delivery system, corporate profitability, and our faith. These are core components of our society. To insure the widespread embrace of video games, a battle must be fought to clear the way for this movement to reach its tipping point. Once this happens nothing can stop it. This is the source of my confidence. This is why we can win.

CHAPTER SIXTEEN
A SOLDiER'S STORY AnD THE
BATTLE FOR THE TiPPinG POinT

While I was writing this book, I did a lot of work in local coffee shops. On many occasions, I would see a person named George Kalergis. George is this jovial, happy go lucky guy that seemed to have his priorities straight. He loved his family and kids and he loved fishing. One day he found out that I was writing a book and we began to have extensive conversations about its content and premise. I could not figure George out. On one hand, he was very supportive of the effort that I was putting forth. But, on the other hand, he would be so aggressive and negative when questioning the possibility of all of this becoming a reality. He kept pressing me on when he could expect to see the rollout of the "killa app" software that would change the world. One day this was really starting to get on my last nerve and I just asked, "Why do you keep riding me for answers to complex questions that could take a lifetime to define?" He then began telling me his story.

As it turns out, George is a retired Army Colonel who spent 25 years in military service, including tours in Vietnam. His assignment was field artillery. He likes to say that his job was to "blow stuff up." As an officer he had the responsibility of making sure that the soldiers under his command had a passion for doing the same.

George's family has a storied military background. His family tree of military service goes all the way back to Sparta in Greek history. His family has been in America for three generations. His father, Lt. General James G. Kalergis joined the Army as a private in 1940 after graduating from Boston College. He then went to officer candidate school (OCS) and against all odds, he progressed through the ranks and in 1965, he received his general's Star. He was most proud that he made General the hard way, the son of immigrants who fought from the bottom to get to the top—only in America.

His son, George, on the other hand, seemed destined to take a revolutionary path. He never quite fit in with the system. He always questioned the status quo; he always challenged obligatory answers as well as rules that seemed to have no relevance to the bottom line. As you could have guessed, he did not fare well in the traditional educational system.

In 1965, after flunking out of four colleges, he was drafted into the Army at age 22. When he finished basic training, he went to officer candidate school just like his father. He was able to successfully complete the curriculum. He still looks back and wonders how he got through. One year to the day he was drafted, he got his papers to go to Vietnam. Ironically, he and his father served in Vietnam at the same time.

In Vietnam, he was given the job of directing artillery fire in response to calls for help from his brothers under fire. Like everyone else, he was scared, but his biggest apprehension was that he would let his fellow GI's down by not being able to do his job. He had a right to be, because according to him, his training "sucked." He only had six months of artillery training. Most of it took place in a classroom and his experience of actually calling in artillery battery fire consisted of three simulated missions. The target was a stationary tank, and no one was shooting at him.

George found himself on the battlefield and his skills were quickly put to the test. After his first fire missions, he began to notice some standards. The time from when he gave coordinates for a target, to the moment he saw the first shot explode was always about 10 minutes, no matter what. This was frustrating because he knew that with every passing minute, more of his brothers in arms were dying. One day he called in the coordinates as usual, and the firebase responded, "on the way" in 30 seconds. A short time later, he saw the ordinance on target. George thought this was nuts. Why could the other batteries not match this standard? He wanted to know how it was done.

He got his chance when he was transferred to another unit where he served as a forward observer. One day, by coincidence while back at base, he found the fire team with the unbelievable efficiency that he had seen earlier. It turns out that the fire direction officer was in Officer Training School with him. He asked his buddy how he achieved such efficiency. His friend said that the team only concentrated on blowing stuff up. They did not care about anything in the procedure book that did not produce speedy fire on target.

George decided that when he became a fire direction officer, his team would do the same, except better. Six months later he got his wish and he took over his own fire direction center. He told his team that they would have the first round on target in less than 30 seconds from call in, and everybody laughed. He had to convince them that this could be done, and how important this goal was. He got rid of the cutting-edge, but seldom-working first generation firing solution computers. He streamlined the procedure by defining which steps were mission-critical and which were not. He also fused many tasks together. Next, he created a simplified manual that would be the bible for every man to follow.

George was successful in getting his team focused on the bottom line, blowing stuff up with speed and accuracy. He used competition and competitive pride to push his team to their limits of excellence and they became one of the best fire batteries in Vietnam. His life's story was beginning to give me insight into George, the man, but I felt that there was more to unveil.

George explained that today he felt he was experiencing a kind of déjà vu. Except this time, he was not facing an enemy in the rice paddies of Vietnam. The new enemy is the current way we teach our children. He felt that his children were caught in a slow, descending spiral and he did not know how to stop the inevitable crash and burn from happening. His daughter, Hailee is 14 and his son, Demitrius is 10. He and his wife have tried every traditional educational avenue, both public and private, and his children are still struggling. Both are supposedly suffering from some form of attention deficit disorder, and neither the public or private system is meeting their needs. George began experiencing the same frustration as when he would call in the coordinates for a fire mission and the first shell would not show up for 10 minutes. For him, the current educational system seems insensitive to achieving what really matters.

Children should receive a foundation that will allow them to pursue interests that they like and that society needs. He feels that in today's world, there is a heavier burden than at any other time in history for curriculums to have relevance and learning style flexibility, but sadly they do not.

George explained that he keeps pushing me for answers because he is impressed with the focus and excitement that video games generate in his kids. He is high on the prospect of harnessing video games for educational purposes and the greater good. He feels that this movement represents an unprecedented approach that he wants to use to help his children. His sense of urgency is spurred by the fear that help will come too late for them and he is determined not to let that happen. In video games, he sees a similarity to the "Aha!" moment he experienced in Vietnam on that fire mission when he saw a round on target in 30 seconds instead of 10 minutes.

My research had proven to him that things could be different. It is amazing how awareness can jump-start momentum toward change. Now his behavior was easier to understand. I am reminded of what former Massachusetts senator "Tip" O'Neil once said, "Politics is always local." Individuals are most strongly motivated when an effort put forth will be directly applied to personal concerns. George's actions are fueled by his desire to learn how we can win *right now*.

We Shall Overcome

During the Civil Rights Movement Dr. Martin Luther King, Jr. had a similar sense of urgency to evoke change. His focus was on racial discrimination. For many, Dr. King's pace for change felt like it was moving at light speed. But for him, it all seemed to be proceeding at a snail's pace.

He was very vocal in expressing his frustration with the process. Even allies pleaded with him to embrace a posture of gradualism. Dr. King discussed this suggestion in one of his most storied orations. He said, "On the subject of how fast should we introduce change, I will respond to my critics by uttering three words. These three little words are: all, here and now." He then elaborated: "We as Negroes today are ready to demand all of our rights and we want all of our rights, here and now." For George, it is no different. He wants his children to have all the opportunities available to succeed in life and he wants the change to happen here and now.

I assured George that he was not alone in his desire to see change, but this is indeed a complex issue. One cannot expect to wake up one morning and find that this problem has gone away. I also cautioned that we must accept the fact that our mortality may prevent us from seeing the ultimate victory. It is imperative that we have a long haul attitude and strategic plan. But once the movement gets started it will no doubt explode like a wildfire. I also reassured him that this was not Vietnam and this was a war that we are going to win. He sharply retorted, "Why Butch? Why are you so confident that we can win this thing?" As usual, he was very doubting, but I convinced him to listen to my rationale.

My confidence is based on three factors. First, I believe in the power of social epidemics that Malcolm Gladwell discussed in the best selling book, *The Tipping Point*. I have great confidence in his explanation of how things that seem subtle can cause great things to happen. Second, I am confident that in the near future, computing hardware/software and connectivity will become a transparent constant in everyone's life. Lastly, I believe in what Barack Obama talked about in his book, *The Audacity of Hope*. He said, "The intangible that has defined this nation has always been its dogged optimism fueled by the boundless exploration of the *what if* that is transformed into *I can,* powered by a catalyst called freedom."

The Tipping Point gripped public attention like a magician captures an audience with a demonstration of the unexplainable being executed right before their eyes. The readers of this best seller could not believe what they were being told. Even the smallest, most subtle factors can cause monumental changes to happen overnight. The three rules of the establishment of social epidemics include: (1) The Law of the Few (2) The Stickiness Factor and (3) The Law of Context. All it takes is a few exceptional people, exalting the virtues of items with catchy allure, properly aligned with current context and circumstance, to cause something to tip.

That is what it takes for something to go from being insignificant to becoming a dominant force in your everyday life. The point in the space-time continuum where something experiences sudden, radical, explosive propagation is called *the tipping point*. The use of video games in mainstream society for the greater good to assist this nation in its quest to continue thriving in an ever-increasing competitive world is about to tip.

The Law of the Few applies today in terms of contributing to the initiation of a social epidemic and video games for the greater good. The number of video game players and their diverse demographic has attained critical mass and leaders are slowly coming forth. I am just one of the *first of a few* that signals the appearance of a horde of champions with world-class credentials, who cannot be disarmed, discredited and explained away.

A united chorus of investigational effort will rapidly squash any remaining pockets of resistance. These leaders, the special carriers of the code, which represents the DNA of a revolution, will spread the call to action to others using the same principles that govern the proliferation of a virus. With viral epidemics, the initial contagion frequently does not stay at the same level of virulence and gets stronger as time goes along. This is what happened with the flu epidemic in 1918. The virus was initially very mild but it quickly transformed into one of the most deadly pathogens known to man. It tipped, and before the world could blink, 40 million people were dead.

I believe that we are poised to have the same type of contagion demonstrated with video games used for the greater good. There are already signs. There is ample evidence of an increasing interest in using video games for corporate training, improving medical care and even in faith-based applications.

The next factor is the unbelievable inherent stickiness factor of video games. Whenever the subject is brought up, whether you are for or against, a visceral response is elicited from the public. The conversation starts and you have to pry yourself away.

Most other issues don't achieve the attraction and notoriety that video games can instantly generate. They represent one of the most formidable branding vehicles known to mankind. Along with the "cool factor," the rapid dissemination of the message to all of society will be executed with an effectiveness on par with the ride of Paul Revere.

Finally, the law of context will contribute to the explosive expansion of the video games for good epidemic. This is driven by desperation of the state of our union. It is akin to a scientific experiment where the culture medium that a pathogen is placed in, can greatly influence its growth rate. We have reached such dire straits in so many facets of our society; even the most conservative experts have to admit what we have been doing is not working and our country today finds itself in a near crisis mode. Regardless, we should not be paralyzed by fear because desperation can be the great facilitator of innovation and change. The power of context facilitates the conversion of factors that cause a crisis to become a primer resulting in small interventions producing rapid monumental changes in our society.

In order for any epidemic to spread, there must be a vehicle that can facilitate efficient exposure to the virus. All modes of transmission are not created equal. Air borne transmission is the most virulent and efficient. This concept can be applied to my explanation of why we can recapture the initiative of this nation through harnessing the power of video games. I believe that in the near future, the widespread availability of computers and connectivity will provide a transparent transmission agent that will accelerate the incorporation of positive video game attributes into mainstream society.

According to data published by the United States Microcomputer Statistics Committee (USMSC), for calendar year 2006, the industry shipped 35,400,535 desktop and workstations computers as well as 23,937,560 notebook computers for a total of 59,338,095 units. Current three-month rolling average sales of these units are tracking at 5.15 million combined units per month with a forecast of the 2007 PC and workstation market increasing 3.1 percent over 2006. Therefore, expected deliveries in this market for 2007 should total approximately 61,175,575 units.

The current population, according to the United States Census Bureau, is 302,419,072. This is based on the 2000 census and national population estimates. This means that at an annual rate of over 61 million PC's shipped per year, we could supply the entire population of the United States with a new computer every five years. With the advent of the $100 dollar computer, the barriers for computer ownership are rapidly melting away. The cost of an Internet-capable personal computer is disappearing as a barrier for even low-income families.

A very strong sign of the coming of ubiquitous connectivity is the fact that some municipalities are setting up low cost wireless networks with ISP provider partners. For example, the city of Dayton, Ohio partnered with provider, Clearwire. For $14.95 per month plus a one-time acquisition of their modem, Dayton citizens have wireless Internet accessibility in the entire city and many surrounding suburbs for either laptops or desktop computers. As of June 2007, 385 cities or counties in the United States have implemented or have free wireless Internet municipal networks in the planning stages.

What we see happening today is not unlike the effort by Andrew Carnegie in 1881 when he decided that one of the greatest contributions that could be made to this nation, still struggling to pull itself out of the shadows of the catastrophic Civil War, was to set up a foundation dedicated to building libraries in every major city in this country (a total of 1,681 libraries were built). The endeavor started a movement to provide free mass access to information to every member of our nation. With great leadership and execution of a sound strategic plan, it is within our grasp in the near future to assure that even the poorest family can have a computer and Internet access. This offers everyone entry into a world of enlightenment, empowerment and unlimited freedom to manifest individual and societal destiny.

Ubiquitous access to computer technology and connectivity amplifies the formula of a social epidemic as stated in *The Tipping Point*. The impact of the law of the few is expanded. In cyberspace, it is possible for more individuals to be exposed to and affected by the charisma of a few great leaders. For the same reason, the impact of the stickiness factor is also exponentially expanded. Ultimately, the individual's appreciation and situational awareness of context is heightened and continuously updated.

The final reason for feeling that victory is within reach comes from the pages of Barack Obama's best selling book, *The Audacity of Hope*. Senator Obama is the Democratic junior senator from Illinois, who is a candidate for President in 2008. Obama presents his vision on how we can move beyond our divisions to tackle the chronic problems of society. I do not agree with all of Senator Obama's beliefs, but you don't have to share identical profiles of opinions and ideals to have common ground.

Like him, I believe in the fundamental decency of the American people. Like him, I believe that "at the core of the American experience is a set of ideals that are able to stir our collective consciousness." Despite our differences, there is a common thread that we all share made up of pride, duty, sacrifice and hope. To my friend George and others, having confidence that Americans will ultimately do the right thing may seem irresponsible and dangerous. Some would say that believing in the inherent goodness of America is only a practice of self-delusion to which we can no longer afford to subscribe.

I would beg to differ because I know why Senator Obama has confidence in his beliefs. All you have to do is look at the history of this nation. There have been two World Wars that we tried hard not to become involved in. As we fulfilled the due diligence that our political process mandates, our division of public opinion and hesitancy to act, was mistaken for weakness by our enemies. In both instances, they grossly underestimated our capacity for oneness. Next, I only have to look at the Civil Rights Movement in this country and review what Martin Luther King was able to do in such a relatively short period of time. These are just a few examples that mandate citizens like Senator Obama, to believe in the fabric of this nation's grit, tenacity, capacity to respond to crisis, and its great capacity to do well.

I also agree with Senator Obama that if you had to quantify "this thing" that defines the American spirit, it would be that at our very core, we all identify with, and have the *audacity to hope*. We dare to believe that no matter what the scoreboard says, that we can overcome any and all obstacles. We can and have a responsibility to dictate our own fate. It is that confidence and audacity that joins us uniquely as a republic.

Combined with the concept of the tipping point, we have amassed a formidable armada to set sail our nation's fortune to a new land of plenty. There are those that feel that I am showing bold confidence bordering on arrogence by predicting how this revolution will spread. But in his book *Technology and The Future of Healthcare: Preparing for the Next 30 Years*, David Ellis states, "The fact is, every human-inspired revolution must have been predicted, otherwise it could not have occurred. The medium is the message. The difficulty is in getting people to listen." With the help of video games, the message will not have a problem being heard.

CHAPTER SEVENTEEN

CASE STUDIES OF A REVOLUTION

As George sat there listening to me talk, I could see that he wanted to believe me, but he was skeptical that all of this could parlay into the real world. At this time, I felt that it was imperative to give examples of how the pendulum of change had limitless applications to other sectors of our society.

Video Games Changing The Face of Healthcare

My first references are examples from healthcare. George was well aware of my incorporation of video games into surgical training to help surgeons learn very difficult procedures with an increase in efficiency and a decrease in errors. But I suggested that video games could influence the delivery of healthcare in a much broader sense. Providing timely, cost-effective, quality healthcare for all is a lofty goal that cannot be accomplished with our current delivery strategies.

It is imperative that we investigate, validate and embrace different methodologies that allow us to do more with limited resources. The fact is that we do not have a healthcare system at all. We have a *sick care* system. Currently, you *cannot get care until you get sick,* and this is much too late. This strategy is one based on retroactive intervention and not proactive measures. The key to extending our healthcare dollar is focusing on wellness and extending our investment in good health beyond the doctor's office and the hospital into our homes and everyday lives. Furthermore, we cannot continue the present path of shouldering an increasing healthcare budget and watching in horror as disparity in service delivery expands unchecked. One of the lynch pins of a successful effort is called telemedicine, which is the delivery of healthcare services with the assistance of providers remotely.

As you would expect, there are other features of our healthcare system that must be modified or changed if we are to achieve our goals. I have called this overall collective strategy to improve healthcare delivery in the 21st century, the Rosser Doctrine.

Features of the Rosser Doctrine for Healthcare in the 21st Century:

- *Execution of a first care delivery strategy facilitated by the mantra, "people should not come to healthcare, but rather healthcare should come to the people."*

- *Establishment of an expanded healthcare provider for the workforce. Empowering non-traditional providers in focused clinical areas of expertise to help deliver care should mobilize people to help take care of themselves. In the military this is referred to as the introduction of a "force multiplier" to the battlefield to overcome a strategic disadvantage in troops or firepower. The public has to shoulder a larger burden in the provision of healthcare in the future. They must become frontline stakeholders in their own wellness destiny. At the same time, physicians and other traditional providers must surrender total dominion over healthcare provision.*

- *Empowering this new frontline healthcare provider can be accomplished by focusing cutting-edge knowledge and skill transfer techniques utilizing digital interactive media.*

- *This new workforce must be technologically savvy and their interface with high-tech appliances must be thinned with an education program that has metrics to dynamically monitor performance.*

- *Using telemedicine will provide care directly or execute oversight and maintenance of quality control and patient safeguards of the non-traditional provider workforce.*

This strategy changes the paradigm of healthcare. It moves away from the current defensive, after the fact, crisis management posture, which is very costly and erodes provider resources. The proposed system embraces a preemptive, preventative medical strategy. It is similar to the first responder CPR program that caused a revolution in cardiac care, except that the Rosser Doctrine is wider in scope.

The execution of the Rosser Doctrine is greatly dependent upon education and training to prepare ordinary people to do extraordinary things. Wherever these items are pivotal to success, video games can play a major role in finding solutions. It is already happening in the healthcare field.

Games for health have begun making an impact in diverse applications. One such area is patient-governed treatment for chronic disease. Titles such as *Spiro Boy* empower children to help determine proper treatment for asthma, and *Gluco Boy* assists in the management of Type I diabetes in children. I would like to now review a real world project that illustrates how video games can impact the facilitation of the Rosser Doctrine. This project is called Operation Beating Heart.

Sudden death for participants in athletic activities is truly a tragic problem. The deaths of children and adults on all levels of competition over the past few years have placed emphasis on the need for better screening of athletes for pre-existing medical conditions. Many of these deaths are caused by cardiac abnormalities.

Preemptive mass screening is the answer, but has been viewed as too costly. Operation Beating Heart *screens all participants with a detailed medical history, physical exam, EKG, pulmonary function study, urinalysis, blood chemistries and an echocardiogram of the heart. All of these screenings are done with the help of regular citizens who have received training in all of the sophisticated measures in a day-and-a-half-long video game assisted training course. Physicians and allied health personnel used telemedicine to oversee their work. This is an extension of historical early cardiac care intervention. Civilian first responders routinely intervene with CPR and they save lives everyday. Today, first responder use of defibrillators has increased the number of lives saved.*

All of this is done without professional medical supervision. Operation Beating Heart *takes this concept to the next level by assisting in the diagnosis of cardiac problems before patients face sudden death. All the core features and principles of the* Rosser Doctrine *are showcased:*

a. *Training of non-traditional providers to conduct evaluations of cardiovascular systems with video game-based training program.*

b. *Using cost-effective, easy-to-use, portable diagnostic and treatment appliances (Cardiac ultrasound, EKG, and Pulmonary Function appliances).*

c. *Implementation of telemedicine (remote care of patients utilizing telecommunications) treatment and oversight protocols while the cardiologists and sonographers are at the hospital.*

This project has already been piloted with success at Savanna State University in Savanna, Georgia and has been the subject of peer-reviewed academic presentations. It is a documented example of how video games can help contribute to changing the way health care is delivered for the better.

The Coffee Chronicles

I have a friend who just started a new job working for a Fortune 500 beverage company. He quickly proved himself to be an effective leader with the gifts of intellect, vision, humility and the ability to inspire. I remember how excited I was for him and his new opportunity. I was at his house playing video games one day with our kids, when I noticed that he seemed distant. I finally stopped playing long enough to inquire what was wrong. He explained that he was very excited about his job and the company was doing extremely well. There was no secret that his company was on top of the mountain, but his concern was how they were going to stay there in the future.

Many others were coming into the space and competition was heating up. He knew that I had done consulting for corporations and he asked my opinion.

I began by asking him to describe the future picture of the company. He stated that their goal was to double the number of stores in the next five years with a heavy concentration on the international market. Wow! I instinctively responded that the number one fear I would have would be maintaining their corporate DNA with such an aggressive expansion goal. This concern was heightened by their focus on the international markets.

By coincidence, during the previous week, I had been in a company store in Mexico. I saw first-hand how there could be nuances of business practice lost in translation. To be successful, I told my friend, his company must concentrate as they move forward to shift focus from the "rat race" of *product innovation*, and focus on *process enhancement*. In view of the company's portfolio of over 700 products, it must temper reliance on the innovation power curve to drive business. This may have worked earlier when the marketplace was all theirs. But, times change and their strategies must also be adjusted. In my opinion, the shift should start with training procedures.

I asked how much they were spending on training and was shocked by the figure. I asked how many hours it took to train an employee. He gave me another shocking figure. Then I asked details about the training process. It consisted of the employee reading a manual and following a trainer around, who happened to be one of the best employees. Then I asked about the yearly turnover rate for employees. I was given yet another shocking figure. The turnover rate was 100 percent in one year, and the majority of the attrition occurred in the first 90 days.

I didn't need to hear anymore. I made the suggestion that their current training model was not optimized for their present business model and certainly would not support their future goals, because it could not expand to scale. First, I suggested, "sit down and read the manual. In-store only training needs to be phased out. Also, the dependence on a training chaperone is absolutely restrictive as it is presently utilized. This results in decreased productivity and ultimately lowers profits."

He quickly stopped me and proudly commented that his company's program was an industry leader. I retorted, "The effectiveness of your training program is not as good as you think it is. Where is your data to support your claim (the scientist in me coming out)? Where is your 'how are we really doing' training report card with reliable metrics?" "Well, we are working on that," he answered. I responded, "This is good because if you can't measure it, you can't manage it."

I continued to explain that being prepared by an inadequate training system, the employees were being thrown to the wolves to sink or swim in a baptism by fire. A vast number of them were not able to make the cut. I suspect that this is the cause of the high turnover of personnel, especially in the early phase of frontline service. The workers are put into a situation with a high likelihood of failure facilitated by customers with a high expectation of quality, accuracy and efficiency. From the beginning, the workers are under pressure to get the order right the first time with a short wait. Sitting down and reading a manual for 40 hours does not prepare you for this.

My friend finally gave up his defensive posture and proclaimed that he got it. He then wanted to know what the next steps should be. I told him that I would not put my money on offering employees more benefits or privileges. I would not suggest starting a massive advertising campaign, and I told him not to start offering more products. Start by executing an innovative 21st century training initiative. This initiative should be based on the utilization of a dynamic, digital, interactive media matrix that fuses entertainment with education to enhance the training process. It should use validated video game-based knowledge and skill transference techniques laced with a heavy influence of pop culture to inspire, recruit, and retain their workers. The process is what I call *stealth learning*.

Stealth learning enhances empowerment and performance through task simulation. It places facts to be learned within an enriched immersive narrative environment. The workers will have a better store readiness because by using this experiential training method, their employees will be able to *practice before they play.*

I asked him what his biggest training issues were. He did not hesitate to say, "frozen beverages." Apparently, efficiency drops off when comparing order time for warm and frozen products. I shocked him when I told him to give me 10 days to place the training information in the manual into a *stealth learning* package. This was going to include both the cognitive information and how to execute the procedure. Most people erroneously believe that video games can only help improve manipulative tasking.

He was very apprehensive about my ability to make good on my claim. In 10 days, he received an e-mail link to the project. His mouth fell open as he went through the tutorial. The manual had been replaced by a virtual chaperone. The facts were transferred without the worker being aware. Facts were important to know, but only in the context of successful execution of the job at hand—making the frozen beverage the proper way, the first time, with a short wait. The video game even had simulated crowd noise and comments from irate customers.

The worker not only had to work against the clock when producing the virtual frozen beverage, the ingredients had to be placed in the right sequence and in the right amount. At the end of the exercise, a report card told how the student performed and critiques were offered on how to improve. The overall scores were not just compared to the local standards but with the standards of other employees around the world.

Needless to say he was stunned. But from my vantage point of having used these techniques to improve performance in surgery, this was child's play and fun. The important thing is that he was excited and his next goal was to take this to leadership and see if their corporate culture was ready to evolve. So, stay tuned for an update in the future on the "Coffee Chronicles."

God at Play: Faith Needs Gamin' Too

That's right! I am prepared to contend that video games will even have a contributory presence in the lives of those of faith. It is my contention that God should be on this playground. The argument can be effectively pursued by responding with three words: predicament, proximity and pivotal.

If we closely examine today's church it finds itself in a serious predicament. The church seems surrounded like Custer at the Little Big Horn with the erosion of such staple assets as character, values and moral absolutes. It is also in desperate need of closer proximity to those for which it is sworn to spread the *good news*. All of this is coming at a pivotal time in the history of the church as an institution and its service to mankind.

On the surface, the prominence and power of faith in today's society may appear to be of unparalleled substance. Leveraging its societal and economic presence, the church even played a strong role in the race for the White House in 2004. There are those that would point to this as the quintessential symbol of the church's influence on our nation and urge the embrace of the conclusion that faith in America is enjoying its finest hour.

But as the church basks in the sunshine of perceived prevalence and prominence, it still struggles to find relevance with the people that it is supposed to serve and save. The barometer of that struggle can be followed by the continuing challenges of its members in the pews. The Church continues to struggle in the transference of moral values of both the personal and societal variety. Further, with many high profile leadership lapses serving as a beacon, many think it is becoming more and more difficult for the church to provide spiritual and moral guidance.

To add to the challenge, children are coming to the church with less of a moral foundation, discipline and plain old manners.

The key to winning this struggle is getting all the souls in the church on the same page and rapidly getting new converts up to speed. This can be most effectively accomplished with communication techniques that facilitate proximity by using tools the public can relate to and understand. Therefore, a common ground must be established which builds a foundation of trust and confidence to allow the flow of effective communication. This is not optional; it is part of a scriptural mandate.

Bishop James Dixon of the Community of Faith Church in Houston, Texas and Reverend Jerry Young, Pastor of the New Hope Baptist Church in Jackson, Mississippi, and First Vice President of the National Baptist Convention, offer the following guiding light from the scripture as to the biblical mandate of proximity with the people in order to spread the word of God. Both feel very strongly that the Bible is clear on this mandate and have brought to my attention a section of scripture that appears to be applicable, I Corinthians 9:18-23.

Paul's first letter to the church at Corinth was tearfully written with a heavy, anguished heart. Paul had come under great duress and microscopic scrutiny, and had endured a year and a half of labored service. His first letter could be considered a summary of his initial effort, and it frames the backslidden state in which the young church there found itself. It is against this backdrop that Paul addresses the faith of the church at Corinth and their current condition.

In the selected scriptures, Paul re-emphasizes the successful strategy that gave him access to the ears of the people, which led to their hearts and souls being won over to the Word. Paul used proximity to those to which the "good news" was to be spread, using icons familiar to the population. He readily admits that he put himself in the shadow of the culture of the diverse minions of people that occupied the city and ministered to them through their ways and interests in order to establish effective communication.

Today's society presents a similar challenge faced by Paul in Corinth in 56 BC. Today, as in Corinth, the proximity of cultural diversity is an extreme constant. Except in today's society, the world is truly flat and that which happens in another part of the world can affect all. Still, just as in Paul's day, the "good news" must still be articulated.

Video games, their practice and methods, have the potential to provide proximity to the people and serve in many faith-based applications. (1) Video games can act as a hook to capture the attention of the believers or potential young believers and draw them into the church. (2) They can also serve to transfer knowledge of the Bible and project an enhanced perception of the life and times of its main characters and circumstances. (3) Churches that seek to be relevant in the lives of the souls they are sworn to gather and oversee can use video games to enlighten, educate and empower the children and membership at large in areas such as general education and issues of community welfare and social responsibility. (4) One the most sophisticated applications involves the rapidly evolving world of social simulation.

Virtual worlds can allow people of faith to face and rehearse real world challenges through the presentation of real life events through simulation. This can help to shape a person's profile of character and moral competency. Mistakes can be made and critiqued without the believer suffering destructive consequences. (5) Finally, social simulations in the virtual world can allow people of faith to form a faith-based global community, which allows collaboration of those of like minds and hearts to address all sorts of contemporary issues on an ongoing basis with expansion of scale.

Some of today's progressive churches are beginning to utilize pop culture icons as "hooks" to bring young people into church. Unfortunately, their use is not coordinated with any goals. They are mainly used as a pacifier and a reward for participating in Sunday school lessons. This can lead to video games being exploited in the church in a fashion that is an extension of misuse at home. This approach is essentially nothing more than a digital baby sitter. Most of the games used are popular over-the-counter titles, and entertainment is their main purpose. I mention this practice as a warning of what not to do.

Video games should only be embraced when they are part of a bigger plan to drive knowledge transfer and to retain God's word, practices and principles. It should not be an add-on to outdated methods of delivering the good news of faith.

EPILOGUE

After hearing all of this, George just leaned back in his chair. I could tell the old warhorse was beginning to soften. But there was one last straw that made him continue to desperately cling to the vestiges of doubt. Much to George's surprise, I then announced that he has to believe in everything that I just said. He looked at me puzzled. I continued by informing him that he had first-hand experience that my formula for change works.

In spite of being baffled by my statement, he allowed me to continue. I asked George to think back to his Vietnam experience and what he was able to do with his fire battery. He used the three elements of *The Tipping Point* to start his own mini-social epidemic to get his team to become the best firing battery in Vietnam. He was the very charismatic leader who successfully executed rule one, the law of the few. He exercised rule two (Stickiness Factor) by rallying the team around the mantra, "we blow stuff up." Finally, he was able to harness the power of context by connecting everyone to what matters most. At all times, each man had lethal focus on putting ordinance on target as quickly as possible to save the lives of their brothers in the field.

The new order tipped and his firing battery became the best in Vietnam, and he led this amazing turnaround in record time. I further reminded George that he, the son of a second-generation immigrant who rose through the ranks of the Army to achieve three General's Stars, was the one who did that. A person who had flunked out of four universities and everybody had given up on. All anyone has to do is to look at his life to see that the impossible is only a transient opinion of outcome that can be breeched by innovation and change driven by the audacity to believe that dreams do come true.

For the first time, I saw those steely eyes soften. He was forced to let go of all his apprehension. At the same moment, I saw in his expression, the face of a nation prepared to rally around maturing all assets at their disposal to take back the initiative and secure its future by all means necessary. Like Senator Obama, George and I feel that we have no choice; it is crunch time. We are in danger of being one of the few generations of Americans that leave behind a weaker and more fractured nation than the one that was inherited. That is a thought that none of us can be comfortable with.

I then put my hand on George's shoulder as I added one last caveat to put this situation in his terms. The platoon is under fire; the coordinates have been identified and sent. The round has been fired and it is on the way. Our job is to spot the location of our first attempts and help to make adjustments to pinpoint the target and then do whatever is necessary to pour on the coals. We can win this thing! Our focus should not be on whether or not we will be victorious. My only concern is echoed in the message that Senator Obama's wife, Michelle relayed to him right before going on stage for his stirring speech at the 2004 Democratic National Convention, when she whispered in his ear, "Just don't screw this up, buddy."

WORKS CITED

BOOKS:

Card, Orson Scott. 1985. *Ender's Game*. New York: Tor Books.

Carson, Ben. 2000. *The Big Picture*. Grand Rapids: Zondervan.

Dixon, Bishop James. 2007. *If God Is So Good, Why Are Blacks Doing So Bad?* New York: LifeBridge Books.

Ellis, David. 2000. *Technology and The Future of Healthcare: Preparing for the Next 30 Years*. San Francisco: Jossey-Bass.

Gladwell, Malcolm. 2002. *The Tipping Point,* Boston: Back Bay Books.

Johnson, Stephen. 2006. *Everything Bad is Good For You,* New York: Riverhead Trade.

Krondorfer, Bjorn. 1992. "Introduction," in Bjorn Krondorfer, ed., *Body and Bible: Interpreting and Experiencing Biblical Narratives*, Philadelphia: Trinity Press International, p. 2.

Mason, John L. 1990. *An Enemy Called Average*. Tulsa: Insight Publishing Group.

Moss Kanter, Rosabeth. 2004. *Confidence: How Winning Streaks & Losing Streaks Begin & End,* New York: Crown Business.

Obama, Barack. 2007. *The Audacity of Hope*. New York: Three Rivers Press.

Prensky, Marc. 2007. *Digital Game-Based Learning,* New York: Paragon House Publishers.

Troeger, Thomas H. 1996. *Ten Strategies For Preaching In A Multi Media Culture*. Nashville: Abingdon Press. p. 19, 85.

JOURNAL ARTICLES:

Rosser, Jr., James C., et. al. 2007. The Impact of Video Games in Surgical Training, *Archives of Surgery*. 142(2): 181-186.

Carter OB. 2006. The weighty issue of Australian television food advertising and childhood obesity. *Health Promot J Austr* 17: 5-11.

Centers for Disease Control and Prevention (CDC). 2006. State-specific prevalence of obesity among adults – United States. *MMWR Morb Mortal Wkly Rep* 55: 985-988.

Cheng, Tsung. 2006. Obesity Is a Global Challenge. *The American Journal of Medicine*, 119: e11.

Valenti, Lisa, Charles, Janice, Britt, Helena. 2006. BMI of Australian general practice patients. *Australian Family Physician* 35: 561-656.

Chew, Gerard, Gan, Seng and Watts, Gerald. 2006. Revisiting the metabolic syndrome. *Med J Aust* 185: 445-9.

Holohan, Anne and Garg, Anurag. 2005. Collaboration online: The example of Distributed Computing. *Journal of Computer-Mediated Communication*, 10(4): article 16.

Ogden, Cynthia, Flegal, Katherine Carroll, Margaret, et al. 2002. Prevalence and trends in overweight among US children and adolescents, 1999-2000," *JAMA* 288: 1728-1732.

Rosenbaum, Michael Leibel, Rudolph. 1998. The Physiology of Body Weight Regulation: Relevance to the Etiology of Obesity in Children. *Pediatrics* 101: 525-539.

MAGAZINE ARTICLES:

China: Dawn of a New Dynasty. *Time*. January 22, 2007.

Thornburgh, Nathan. Drop Out Nation. *Time*. April 9, 2006.

MOVIES:

Top Gun. 1986. Directed by Tony Scott, Paramount Pictures.

Scary Movie 4. 2006. Directed by David Zucker, Dimension Films.

Star Wars. 1977. Directed by George Lucas, 20th Century Fox.

War of the Worlds. 2005. Directed by Steven Spielberg, Paramount Pictures.

REPORTS

2006 Video Game Report Card. http://www.mediafamily.org/research / report_vgre_2006.shtml.

McKinnon, Jesse. "The Black Population in the United States: March 2002," U.S. Census Bureau, Current Population Reports, Series P20-541 (2003), Washington, D.C.

U.S. Department of Health and Human Services, Office of the Surgeon General. The Surgeon General's Call to Action to Prevent and Decrease Overweight and Obesity. Rockville, MD: US Department of Health and Human Services; (2001).

"World of Warcraft: The Burning Crusade shatters day-1 sales record," Blizzard Entertainment press release, March 7, 2007. Retrieved March 12, 2007.

"World of Warcraft surpasses 8 million subscribers worldwide," Blizzard Entertainment press release, January 11, 2007.

TELEVISION SHOWS:

Ben Casey, M.D. 1961. James Moser, John Pommer, Matthew Rapf, Wilton Schiller, Jack Laied, Irving Elman, ABC.

Gunsmoke. 1955-1975. John Metson, Creator. CBS.

Jeopardy. 1964. Merv Griffin, Creator. NBC.

Lost in Space. 1965. Irvin Allen, Producer. CBS.

Sesame Street. 1969. Joan Ganz Cooney and Sesame Street Workshop Staff, Creators. NET, PBS.

Sleeper Cell. 2005. Clark Johnson, Ziad Doueiri, Showtime.

Star Trek. 1966. Gene Roddenberry, NBC.

St. Elsewhere. 1982. Joshua Brand, John Falsey, Creators. NBC.

The Jetsons. 1962. Hanna Barbera Productions, ABC.

VIDEO AND BOARD GAMES:

America's Army. U.S. Army, 2002.

Asteroids. Atari, Inc. 1979.

Burger Time. Data East Corporation, 1982.

Centipede. Rosenthal, 1981.

Dance Dance Revolution. Konami, 1998.

Donkey Kong. Nintendo, 1981.

Doom. id Software, 1993.

Gluco Boy. Nintendo, 2006.

Grand Theft Auto. ASC Games, 1997

Grand Turismo. Sony, 1997.

Halo 2. Microsoft, 2004.

Lunar Lander. DEC, 1993.

Making History. Muzzy Lane Software, 2006.

MediEvil 2. Sony, 1998.

Ms. Pacman. Midway, 1981.

Operation. Milton Bradley, 1965.

Pong. Atari, Inc. 1972.

Rainbow Six. Red Storm Entertainment, 1998.

Silent Scope (practice mode). Konami, 1999.

Star Wars Racer: Revenge. Lucas Arts, 2002.

Spiro Boy. Nintendo.

Super Monkey Ball. Sega, 2001.

WEB SITE ARTICLES

Becker, David. "Online game makers seek key to profits." http://www.news.com/2100-1040-823258.html, January 25, 2002.

DeMaria, Rusel "Games For Health 2006: Dance Dance... Revolution in Fitness!" http://seriousgamessource.com/features/feature_051906.php.

Gibbons, Michael. "The Year In Numbers," 2004 Profiles of Engineering and Engineering Technology Colleges. http://www.asee.org/publications/upload/2004ProfileIntro2.pdf, May 2005.

Grebski, Wes. "Engineering Technologies Program: Challenges and Opportunities." 2004 Profiles of Engineering and Engineering Technology Colleges, May 2005. http://www.asee.org/publications/profiles/upload/2004ETprofile.pdf.

Mohasseb, Saeed. "Titanic wave of collaborative competition. Are You Fit to Survive? The CEO Refresher" -. http://www.refresher.com/Archives/!titanicwave.html.

Washington, Valarie. "A Look Inside the Strategic Mind." http://ezinearticles.com/?A-Look-Inside-the-Strategic-Mind&id=161741.

"ESRB Statement Regarding 2005 Mediawise Video Game Report Card." Press Release. www.esrb.org/about/news/downloads/mediawise_response.pdf, 2005.

"Facts – Applicants, Matriculants and Graduates." American Association of Medical Colleges. http://www.aamc.org/data/facts/archive/famgloisa.htm.

History of the Human Genome Project. http://www.ornl.gov/sci/techresources/Human_Genome/project/hgp.shtml.

"The Online Game Market Heats Up." http://www.dfcint.com/game_article/june04article.html, June 30, 2004.

WEB SITES

Body Mechanics. http://www.bodymechanics.tv/ParentZone/DVDPack.html

ChangeMakers. "Competitions." http://www.changemakers.net/en-us/competitions

"Collaboration." http://en.wikipedia.org/wiki/Collaboration

"Competition." http://en.wikipedia.org/wiki/Competition

WORKS CITED

Second Life. http://en.wikipedia.org/wiki/Second_Life

Second Life. "What is Second Life?" http://secondlife.com/whatis/

Printed in the USA
CPSIA information can be obtained
at www.ICGtesting.com
JSHW082200140824
68134JS00014B/346